IT HAPPENED IN

VIRGINIA

It Happened In Series

IT HAPPENED IN
VIRGINIA

Emilee Hines

TWODOT®

Guilford, Connecticut
An imprint of The Globe Pequot Press

A · TWODOT® · BOOK

Copyright © 2001 by The Globe Pequot Press

The publisher gratefully acknowledges Willima B. Obrochta, Head of Educational Services, Virginia Historical Society, for reviewing this manuscript for historical accuracy.

Cover art © 2001 by Lisa Harvey, Helena, Montana.

Library of Congress Cataloging-in-Publication data is available.

ISBN 0-7627-1166-3

Manufactured in the United States of America
First Edition/Second Printing

Contents

Preface

Virginia is a beautiful state, with almost one-third of its area protected in state or national forests or parks. Virginia has barrier islands, seacoast, coastal plains, piedmont, mountains, and valleys. Throughout the state are historic buildings and battlefields.

Virginia was the site of the first permanent English settlement in North America (Jamestown) and was for the next 200 years the most populous colony and state. But war, economic changes, and the westward movement changed that.

The first settlers encountered Powhatan Indians, members of the Algonquin Nation. As settlers moved westward and northward, they met other tribes as well. Some of the most beautiful place-names in Virginia, such as Shenandoah and Chesapeake, come from Native American words. Today, two tribes still own reservations in King William County, the Mattaponi and the Pamunkey.

In King James I's original land grant to the London Company in 1609, the territory of Virginia stretched north and south of Point Comfort on the Atlantic Ocean for 200 miles, then west and northwest to the Pacific Ocean, encompassing three-quarters of the present United States and much of what is now Canada. After England relinquished the area west of the Mississippi in 1763, Virginia still included territory northwest to the Great Lakes. Virginia gave up claims to this vast Northwest Territory when it joined the other former colonies to form the United States of America.

Geologically, Virginia has some unusual formations—Natural Bridge, Natural Tunnel, and Natural Chimneys—where ancient seas once washed and shaped the limestone. In Fairystone State Park in Henry County, crystals in petrified wood have produced small crosses that are used as jewelry. Virginia has iron ore at Ferrum, bauxite at various locations, and huge deposits of coal in its western mountains. Until the California gold strike in 1849, Virginia's Goochland and Buckingham Counties were America's leading producers of gold.

Both the Revolutionary War and the Civil War were fought extensively in Virginia, and the surrenders that ended both these wars took place in Virginia. Although Virginia is considered a conservative state and was the capital of the Confederacy, Virginia voters in 1989 elected the first African American governor, L. Douglas Wilder.

The history of Old Dominion is colorful and dramatic. *It Happened in Virginia* takes a look at thirty-three historical events that were important in shaping Virginia into the modern state it is today. Some of these incidents are amusing, some are shocking, all are important and make for good reading.

I wish to thank Barnabas Baker, Portsmouth Public Library; Joyce Williams, Kirn Memorial Library, Norfolk; David Spencer, Roanoke Public Library; Ann Kinken Johnson, librarian of *The Virginian-Pilot;* Robin K. Rountree, director of Riddick's Folly, Suffolk; Shenandoah Valley Research Station; and Margaret Hines, Kerry Hines, and Lucy C. Alexander, who all helped with research.

I especially want to thank my husband, Thomas B. Cantieri, who patiently read my manuscripts, made suggestions, and endured many microwaved frozen dinners while I worked on this book.

A Tragic Beginning
· 1607 ·

Three wooden ships, *Susan Constant, Godspeed,* and *Discovery,* pitched and lurched in the stormy Atlantic Ocean. The sails shuddered, and between flashes of lightning the Englishmen onboard could see waves almost as high as the ships themselves. The comet that had streaked across the sky on the first day of the new year had earlier predicted their doom. Now, fearing death, they fell to their knees, crying and praying for deliverance.

Finally, the storm ended, and at dawn on April 26, 1607, they spotted the low-lying coastline of Virginia. They dropped anchor in a broad, tranquil body of water later to be named Chesapeake Bay. They went ashore, planted a cross, said prayers of gratitude, and began to explore.

The bay was full of fish and shellfish. Life would be easy here, the Englishmen thought. First one man, then another, and finally a third opened oysters and found pearls. What a land they'd come to! They could get rich just by opening and eating oysters. Besides the bounty from the water, there was plenty of land for the taking, and there must be gold somewhere. After all, the Spanish had found gold in the New World.

One afternoon Indians emerged from the woods and ran at them, shooting arrows. Two men were wounded. The Englishmen fired their muskets, frightening off the attackers. Perhaps life in the New World would not be so easy. They definitely needed to protect themselves against any more attacks.

That night the settlers opened the box of instructions they had brought from King James. Inside was a list of the names of the seven chosen leaders. One of the seven was Captain John Smith, who had been put in chains for causing trouble on the ship. Only twenty-seven years old and just over five feet tall, Smith was a skilled mapmaker and a brave soldier, but he had a violent temper.

Smith demanded to be unchained so that he could take his place as a leader to deal with the Indians and begin mapping Virginia. Smith may have been the king's choice, but his fellow settlers feared him, so they kept him in chains for five more weeks before setting him free.

Over the next several days the settlers met more Indians and were taken to meet the chieftains. Although the settlers believed the Indians to be friendly, they decided to move away from the coast to build their settlement in a safer and more easily defendable place.

They sailed 60 miles up a great river, which they named James in honor of the king, until they came to what they thought was the perfect spot to establish a colony. It was almost an island, attached to the mainland only by a narrow strip of land. It would be easy to defend. They named the place Jamestown.

The weather was wonderful, as springtime in Virginia can be. Flowers were in bloom, birds fluttered about, and most important, they were safe and off the ship. They had arrived at a good time of year for planting.

After clearing trees from the land, the settlers went to work planting wheat and vegetables, making fishing nets, and building houses and a fort. The triangular fort was made of stout logs set into the ground and had a strong gate and small openings where sentries could watch for attackers.

In spite of this good beginning, trouble soon began in Jamestown. In early June, Captain Christopher Newport led a group up the James River to "the falls" (now the site of Richmond). When they returned they found that Indians had attacked the fort, killing two men. Another settler had been taken prisoner, tortured, and burned.

On June 20 Captain John Smith was freed. He set out to explore the bays and inlets of eastern Virginia and produced very accurate maps of the area. He also met the Powhatan Indians and nearly lost his head. According to legend, the chief's daughter, Pocahontas, persuaded her father to spare Captain Smith.

That summer was very dry, so crops shriveled and the water level in the river dropped. One of the settlers wrote, "At high tide, the water is very salty, at low tide full of slime and filth." This was the settlers' drinking water.

The settlers' method of governing the colony added to their problems. The organizers had decided that everything would be shared equally. As a result, lazy men did little work, knowing that they would still share in whatever food others produced. This led to fights, one murder, and eventually starvation.

During the first winter, fire destroyed most of the fort and all but three houses. Gone were food, supplies, and clothing. The years 1609 and 1610 were so difficult that the settlers referred to them as "The Starving Time."

At one low point in June of 1610, the remaining settlers boarded ships to return to England and give up the colony. Their new governor had not yet arrived, and supplies were desperately low. They headed down the James River and were at the mouth of the bay when ships were sighted. If the colonists had left a day earlier or the supply ships had arrived a day later, they would have missed each other on the open sea. Jamestown survived, but its troubles were far from over.

Tobacco: Saving and Destroying Virginia
·1612·

The Jamestown settlers were not surprised that the Virginia Indians smoked tobacco. After all, Christopher Columbus had been offered tobacco and had introduced it to Europe, where it quickly became popular. The Spanish rolled their tobacco into cigars, the Portuguese and some English preferred pipes, and other Englishmen snorted the powdered tobacco (snuff) right into their noses.

Although tobacco was said to cure almost everything—epilepsy, headaches, constipation, asthma, bronchitis, and dropsy—and to improve the memory, it had its enemies, some of them fanatical. In Russia smoking was declared a mortal sin by the church, and smokers were sent to Siberia. The Mogul emperor of India ordered that the lips of smokers be slit, and in China tobacco importers were beheaded. Scientists in England recognized early on that tobacco was deadly, showing the blackened lungs of deceased smokers as proof. Even King James I wrote a treatise against tobacco, calling it "lothsome to the eye, hatefull to the nose, harmfull to the braine, dangerous to the lunges." He could not stop his subjects from smoking, but he could tax tobacco. The price of a pound of Spanish tobacco was already more than two weeks' wages for the average working man, and to this was added a stiff tax of six shillings, ten pence.

After discovering that the Jamestown area had no gold, diamonds, or other valuable minerals, the settlers looked for some agricultural products to support the colony and pay for the manufactured goods they would need. They extracted resin from pine trees to caulk their ships and cut the tall trees to make ship masts. They tried growing silkworms, wine grapes, indigo, cotton, oranges, olives, and sugar, all of which failed.

Then John Rolfe, better known as the husband of Pocahontas, noticed that the Indian tobacco grew well in Virginia but had a sharp taste. In 1612, he imported seeds of the Spanish variety from Trinidad and grew both kinds, side by side. Both grew well, but the Spanish variety clearly tasted better. Rolfe experimented with various methods to cut and cure the crop, and in 1613 he shipped his first load of tobacco to England. It was a financial success. Tobacco was in great demand by the eager London merchants, and soon colonists were planting tobacco everywhere, even in the streets of Jamestown.

In 1616 only 2,500 pounds of tobacco were produced in America. Ten years later, production was 500,000 pounds. Soon the London Company, which sponsored Virginia's first settlers, saw the potential in tobacco, and instead of forbidding its cultivation encouraged it and even protected it.

Tobacco growing is a tedious process that requires a lot of hand labor. In the winter the tiny seeds—a teaspoon can hold 10,000 seeds—are planted in a special bed in fine soil and covered to protect them against frost. As the weather warms and the plants grow, the cover must be removed, at first briefly and then for longer periods of time, so that the plants will have adjusted to strong sunlight by the time they are transplanted to an open field. The colonists had to do the field planting by hand, making a hole for each individual plant and setting the plants nearly two feet apart in hills and rows.

Tobacco pulls a lot of nutrients from the soil, so any competing weeds must be removed. When flower buds appear at the top of the plant, they are broken off so the leaves will grow thick and broad. If the plant is allowed to bloom, it will become tall and scraggly, with narrow leaves. At the junction of each leaf of the plant, small shoots or "suckers" appear, which also have to be broken off. This also ensures that the lower leaves develop. At any stage in their growth, something bad can happen to the plants. Hornworms feast on the plants, eating from underneath the leaf. These have to be picked off by hand and destroyed.

Virginia's early tobacco farmers anxiously watched the sky throughout the summer. Lack of rain meant small plants, and because tobacco sold by the pound, every bit of extra weight helped. If there was too much rain the delicate plants would be washed away or go limp and be burned when the sun came out. Most dreaded of all was a hailstorm. Within minutes the sky could turn a yellowish green and balls of ice would pelt the plants to bits, destroying a season's crop.

As summer went on, the plants at Jamestown grew shoulder high, and in August entire plants were cut and laid out to dry. Eventually Rolfe experimented with hanging the cut plants so air could get to them on all sides and dry them more quickly, and later he began to hang the tobacco plants in barns and applied smoke to dry them.

One court case of the day involved Sir George Yeardley's overseer, who was punished for negligence in harvesting tobacco: "Hee did hang the tobacco so thick upon the lynes that the lynes broke and the tobacco fell to the ground and before the said tobacco was all dryed he make it up into a role and so by his faulte it was wett and not merchantable."

For shipping to England, the dried leaves were stripped off the plants, packed in large barrels called hogsheads, and rolled to the nearest dock to be loaded onto a ship. (Hence many roads in the southern colonies were named Rolling Road.) In England an agent would see to the sale, take his commission, and buy the manufactured goods the Virginians wanted. Tobacco thus became the medium of exchange. Taxes and purchases were always priced in pounds of tobacco; soldiers, officials, and ministers were paid in tobacco. Conducting a funeral cost 400 pounds of tobacco. A wedding cost only half as much!

Because it was profitable and because it soon ruined the field it was planted in, the "vile weed," as King James described it, saved the Virginia colony from bankruptcy and failure but caused many fertile fields to wash into the rivers, sending their owners west. Farmers with large plantations could plant tobacco in a certain field for several years and then clear more land and plant elsewhere, but this was not possible for small farmers.

Because so much hand labor was needed to grow tobacco, indentured servants, African slaves, and criminals were brought to Virginia to work the fields, increasing the population and altering the makeup of the colony. Thus John Rolfe and his Spanish tobacco seeds forever changed Virginia.

Wives and Servants
for Sale
· 1619 ·

When word came one day in 1619 that a ship had been sighted, the single men of Virginia bathed, shaved, dressed in their tattered best, and made their way to the dock. Onboard the ship were ninety women, single, "honestly educated" women who had crossed the Atlantic to be their wives. According to instructions, the women were intended for the "most industrious and honest planters." Probably most Virginia men thought they fit that description. A planter could take a wife by paying for her passage with tobacco.

The Virginia men no doubt fantasized about the women who were soon to arrive. Would there be enough women to go around? What if a man was rejected?

Onboard the ship, the women must have had mixed feelings: relief that the long, harrowing voyage was over and they were about to arrive safely in Virginia, but apprehension about what lay ahead. These women were mostly daughters of parents who had no money for dowries, so their chances for marriage in England were limited. In Virginia, however, women were in demand. An informal 1616 census conducted by John Rolfe had shown that Virginia had an estimated 351 inhabitants, only 65 of whom were women and children.

After arriving in Virginia, all the women soon wed. One of the women, Cecily Johnson, threw the colony into an uproar by promising to marry two suitors. There is no record of how the matter was settled; perhaps there was a duel. More likely she was forced to give up one and choose the other. With the lack of available women in Virginia, it is likely that this type of situation occurred more than once. William Byrd once wrote that a spinster in Virginia was so rare as to be "as ominous as a shooting star."

The men who chose wives from the shiploads of women were doubly blessed: if they paid the passage of a new settler, they were also granted an additional 50 acres of land. What a bargain! They had acquired land and a wife with no need for backbreaking hours of work, a lengthy courtship, or a chat with a father.

The reason the London Company, the sponsor of Virginia's first settlers, gave for sending the women was to make the men feel more at home in Virginia. The belief was that if the men had to provide for wives and children, they would feel more tied to the colony. The company required that the young women be educated and from good families. In Virginia, they were to be married to the most industrious and honest of planters, who could pay for their passage and provisions. The cost was 120 pounds of tobacco per maiden.

Once in Virginia, the young women were to be placed in the homes of married couples of good reputation until they were wed. The women were not to be forced into marriage.

Slaves came to Virginia by the shipload as well. The first African slaves in Virginia were twenty men who had been captured and enslaved in Africa, then brought to Jamestown on August 30, 1619, in a Dutch pirate ship disguised as a man-of-war. In Virginia they were sold to whoever paid the highest price in pounds of tobacco. Two more Africans were brought to Virginia as slaves between 1620 and 1624, although slavery was not officially sanctioned in the colony until 1661, when it was legalized.

During the colony's first years, before the slave trade became entrenched, much of the labor was done by indentured servants. Whoever paid the passage of the indentured person received his or her labor for five to seven years. At the end of that time, the indentured person was freed and was given either 50 acres of land or the tools of a trade to earn a living.

The ship *Jonathon* arrived in June 1620. Among the 200 passengers were "many maids for wives." A few weeks later the *London Merchant* brought more single women, and in 1621 *Marmaduke, Warwick,* and *Tiger* arrived with cargoes of single women.

An Uprising and a Savior
· 1622 ·

For most Virginians, Good Friday, March 22, 1622, dawned peacefully. The settlers went about their business, building fires to drive away the early morning chill, slicing bacon for breakfast, getting dressed, tending to their livestock, unaware of Indians creeping stealthily through the woods toward them.

Suddenly, at 8:00 A.M., disaster struck. Before the day ended, more than 350 settlers—including seven members of the governing council—had been slaughtered, nearly one-third of the population of Virginia. One of the victims was John Rolfe, who had given the colony its cash crop, tobacco, and whose marriage to Pocahontas had brought about a peaceful relationship with the local Indians.

Powhatan, father of Pocahontas, had ruled his tribe wisely and peacefully. The colony probably could not have survived the Starving Time of 1609 and 1610 without the help of the Powhatan Indians. But Chief Powhatan had died, and his brother, Opechancanough, had become the new ruler. He hated the settlers, who continued to move onto his tribe's land, but pretended to be friendly.

The colonists felt secure. They traded with the Indians, sometimes selling them guns and ammunition. They had begun building a college to train Indian boys along with settlers' children at Henrico. When the new governor, Francis Wyatt, had arrived in Virginia late in 1621, he had "solemnly ratified" a peace treaty with the Indians, and a newly arrived minister had built an English-style house for Opechancanough.

But peace ended abruptly that Good Friday morning. Throughout the colony, from Jamestown to the falls (now Richmond), whites were slaughtered. No Africans were killed. Opechancanough reserved his fury for the whites, and his followers carried out the massacre with precision timing, striking all over the colony simultaneously.

Men who had gone out to milk cows or feed horses may have heard a slight rustle in the woods and turned, only to be attacked by well-armed Indians. Clubs crushed skulls and tomahawks broke arms flung up in defense. Mothers nursing babies or dressing children for the day had their babies torn from their arms before their throats were slit and their scalps sliced off. Some of the bodies were dismembered and parts carried away by triumphant Indians.

At Henrico, twenty-two whites were killed and the college under construction was burned. At Falling Creek, farther up the James River, twenty-seven died, and the newly established iron works was destroyed. Berkeley Hundred, site of the first Thanksgiving in America, was almost wiped out.

At Shirley Hundred, on the north side of the James, Nathaniel Causey was severly wounded but managed to cut off the hand of one of his attackers with an axe. The others fled. Causey survived and was later elected to the legislative assembly in 1624.

The Virginia colony would have been completely destroyed if it had not been for the courage of Chanco, a young Indian boy. He was living with Richard Pace at a plantation across the river from Jamestown. When the attack was being planned, Chanco's brother assigned him the job of killing Pace, but Chanco could not bring himself to do it. Pace, he said later, had treated him like a son. The night before Good Friday, Chanco tossed and turned mulling over the horror to come the next day. Finally, unable to endure the dreadful secret any longer, he shook Pace awake and told him what was about to happen.

Pace got up, dressed hurriedly, and rowed 3 miles across the river to Jamestown to warn the governor. The fortress was prepared for attack, with armed sentries placed on duty. Riders and runners hastened in all directions to warn the settlers. As they spurred on their horses or bent to the oars, they must have wondered if they, too, would be caught unaware and struck down from behind.

Despite these efforts, many settlements were annihilated before the warning reached them. At Martin's Hundred, only 7 miles from Jamestown, seventy-six people were killed, and at Edward Bennett's plantation fifty-two were slain. Throughout the colony, the Indians drove off livestock, stole food, and burned houses and crops.

Mrs. Alice Proctor, described by her neighbors as a modest gentlewoman, was apparently a good shot as well. Her husband John was away, but she managed to drive off the attacking Indians and save herself and her family.

Jamestown was saved, although the attack reached Archer's Hope, 5 miles away, where five were slain. Governor Wyatt ordered all survivors to move to Jamestown for their own safety. Mrs. Proctor refused. She had protected herself once and could do so again. Only after the governor's soldiers threatened to burn her house with her in it did she grudgingly move.

The Powhatan uprising was devastating to Virginia. Spring planting was just beginning, but because the settlers had to live at Jamestown they couldn't plant on their own land. Their livestock was gone, which meant no milk, meat, or eggs. They were faced with starvation once more, and this time there were no friendly Indians to help them. By the end of the next winter, 500 more Virginians had died, succumbing easily to disease in their weakened condition.

The survivors organized hunting parties to take revenge, killing Indians and burning their crops and villages. Opechancanough survived to attack Jamestown again, twenty-two years later, on Holy Thursday, April 18, 1644. Still burning with hatred for the whites, he had himself carried into battle on a litter and had his eyes propped open so that he could watch the destruction of his enemies.

This time Opecancanough was captured and taken to Jamestown. The governor intended to send him to England, but a soldier shot him, and the Powhatan tribe made peace with the white settlers. More Virginians were killed in this second attack (nearly 500) because there was no Chanco to give a warning. However, by this time many more immigrants had come to Virginia, so the colony was too strong to be wiped out.

The First American Revolution
· 1676 ·

In 1676, a hundred years before the Revolutionary War, a dashing, charismatic young Englishman, newly arrived in Virginia, led a rebellion against royal authority. Some call Bacon's Rebellion the first American revolution.

The previous decade had been disastrous for Virginia. The population had grown to 40,000, but most of the inhabitants were desperately poor. Storms in 1667 had destroyed more than 10,000 homes, laid waste to two-thirds of the crops, and killed many farm animals. England and Holland were at war in Europe, and this affected Virginia. In 1673 the Dutch seized eleven ships loaded with Virginia tobacco, the colony's cash crop. In that same year a plague wiped out half the cattle that had survived the earlier storms. White settlers along the frontier had killed five Susquehannock chieftans and the Indians had retaliated.

The governor, Sir William Berkeley, was not to blame for any of the catastrophes, but many Virginians resented him. Once popular, he had ruled Virginia for more than thirty years and had become increasingly more tyrannical.

When the House of Burgesses met in Jamestown in March 1676, more than 300 settlers had already been killed by Indians in that year. Settlers on the frontier lived in terror. Instead of sending soldiers to protect them, Governor Berkeley decided to build a series of forts along the frontier. These were useless, the settlers said, because the Indians easily could avoid them. They also protested against being taxed to pay for the forts and having to man the forts instead of defending their own homes. They were right about the uselessness of the forts; by the end of May another 200 settlers had been killed.

The citizens of Charles City County petitioned Governor Berkeley for help. When he refused, they turned to Nathaniel Bacon, then only twenty-eight years old. Bacon, a graduate of Cambridge University in England who was trained as a lawyer, had come to Virginia with his new bride two years earlier. He was kin to an older Nathaniel Bacon, a member of the governing council, and he was a cousin of Governor Berkeley. Within two months of his arrival, the popular and well-connected Bacon had been appointed to the council.

In 1676 Bacon defied the governor. The people on the frontier deserved protection, he thought. When the governor refused him a commission to attack the Susquehannock Indians, Bacon announced that he would attack with or without a commission. Bacon, along with many other Virginians, suspected that Berkeley was profiting so handsomely from fur trade with the Indians that he would never fight them. However, it is likely that Governor Berkeley did not attack the Indians because he did not want to involve the British Empire in a costly war with the local tribes.

Bacon gathered a little army and marched them to the Roanoke River, where the Susquehannocks had a fort. The leader of the Occaneechee Indians, who also wanted to get rid of the Susquehannocks, had asked for Bacon's help in attacking the fort. The joint attack was successful, but after it the Occaneechee chief refused food to Bacon's men and held them on an island. When one of Bacon's men was shot during what was supposed to be a friendly talk, Bacon savagely turned on the Occaneechees and killed more than a hundred.

Governor Berkeley expelled Bacon from the council and charged him with treason for daring to disobey his royal authority. Bacon was captured and brought to Jamestown. Acting on an uncle's advice, Bacon bowed before Governor Berkeley, admitted his guilt, and begged forgiveness for himself and his followers. The governor pardoned the group, reinstated Bacon on the council, and promised him a commission to fight the Indians. Bacon was delighted.

Within a few weeks, however, when no commission had been granted, Bacon realized that he had been tricked and that his life was probably in danger. He slipped out of Jamestown just ahead of the governor's troops, who were searching for him.

Bacon returned with a hundred armed followers and surrounded the capital, demanding his commission. This time he got it, along with commissions for his followers; a letter sent to the king approving his actions; and a series of changes in Virginia's government, known as "Bacon's Laws." These included allowing all freemen, not just landowners, to vote. Church vestries, which had been lifelong appointments, were to be elected every three years. Council members were required to pay taxes like other citizens, officials who overcharged fees were to pay penalties, and each man was allowed to hold only one office. These changes were radical a century before most Americans demanded them.

Satisfied, Bacon once more left Jamestown to attack the Indians. Suddenly, Berkeley changed direction again, declared Bacon and his 1,300 followers traitors, and sent an army against them. When the militia refused to support Berkeley, he fled to the Eastern Shore.

Bacon was now in charge in Virginia, but his followers realized that they had started a civil war. When Bacon tried to get an oath from them to fight any troops sent from England to defend the governor, many refused. Fighting Indians was one thing, but fighting against the royal governor was something else: treason. They changed their minds when word came that the governor had removed all the arms and ammunition from York Fort, leaving the settlers defenseless.

Bacon commandeered two ships to sail to the Eastern Shore and capture Berkeley. But while Bacon was fighting Pamunkey Indians on the mainland, Berkeley's troops captured the two ships and 250 of Bacon's men. Triumphantly, the governor sailed back to Jamestown.

Bacon refused to give up. He fortified the point near Jamestown where the peninsula joins the mainland, using the wives of Berkeley's followers as human shields until trenches were dug. When Bacon's men fired on the capital, Berkeley's troops deserted. Four days later, the wily governor slipped out of Jamestown and once more fled to the Eastern Shore.

Bacon was in control, but word came that a force was being raised in northern Virginia to attack him. If he went north to fight and left the capital unguarded, Berkeley could capture Jamestown. His solution was to leave nothing for Berkeley to take. After removing and safely storing the colony's records, Bacon set fire to the major buildings in Jamestown.

It's difficult to say how the conflict would have ended if Bacon had continued fighting. Perhaps royal authority would have been overthrown in Virginia and independence from England won a century early. We'll never know, because Bacon died in October 1676 of dysentery and fatigue. His followers buried him in an unmarked grave, fearing that Berkeley would desecrate the body. Without Bacon, his army deteriorated.

Berkeley had Bacon's followers hunted down, and he hanged twenty-three of them. Word of the rebellion had by this time reached the king, who had sent three commissioners to investigate. He sent pardons for all the rebels but Bacon. The commissioners and pardons arrived in mid-winter 1677, six months after the rebels had been put to death.

The Incredible Journey
·1755·

Mary Draper Ingles acted so bravely that she became a legend not only to her own people but to the Indians who captured her and held her hostage. In July 1755, Mary was twenty-three years old, married, the mother of two sons, and pregnant with her third child. She lived at Draper's Meadow, the western edge of English settlement, with her husband William, her sons, and her mother.

Virginia was still an English colony, and England was at war with France. France's Indian allies, from their villages in Ohio, attacked English settlers freely along the frontier at the instigation of the French. Mary was captured during one of the nearly 2,000 Indian attacks on frontier settlements during the French and Indian War. Her capture was quite dramatic.

Mary was at home that hot morning of July 8, 1755, while her husband and her brother, Johnny Draper, worked in the fields nearby. Her mother had taken the two boys to pick berries out of sight of the cabin. Suddenly Mary heard a scream from her sister-in-law, Bettie Draper. Before Mary could go inside for a weapon, Bettie ran into the clearing with her baby, pursued by twenty Indians.

They caught up with Bettie and clubbed her, breaking her arm. They grabbed her baby and tossed it back and forth like a toy before dashing it against the cabin wall. Mary and Bettie screamed and fought, but they were helpless against the twenty warriors. Within minutes they were both bound and flung over horses.

Mary silently prayed that her mother and sons would stay away from the cabin, but she saw them come into the clearing. A moment too late they saw the Indians and fled. They were quickly captured. Mary watched helplessly as her mother was tomahawked and scalped, and her sons, Georgie and Thomas, were taken captive.

The women's screams brought their husbands running from the fields, but they arrived without weapons and could only stand in concealment and watch their families be taken away. By the smoke that rose above the trees, they knew they were not the only victims. Three other homes at Draper's Meadow were attacked that day and their occupants killed.

As the group rode westward the women were eventually unbound. Mary tended Bettie's broken arm and took care of her sons while trying to remember some of the landmarks they were passing. If she could escape, she would try to return to Draper's Meadow. But nothing along the route was familiar, for no white women had passed this way before.

On the trail, the Indians paused only long enough for Mary to give birth to a daughter. As weak as she was, Mary had to continue walking westward. She had forced herself not to cry out during childbirth, and now she refused to complain. Her stoicism earned her the grudging respect of her captors.

After several weeks of traveling, the group arrived at an Indian settlement in what is now Ohio. The village was full of captives. Most adults had to run the gauntlet, being clubbed almost senseless before reaching the end. Mary did not, and she soon realized that an Indian planned to make her his wife. She rebuffed him and was put to work along with Indian women. To her dismay, her sons seemed to like being with the Indians and were quickly picking up Indian skills and games.

As fall came, the Indians separated, and the Virginia prisoners were divided. Mary's sons were taken by a chieftain. An

Indian brave led the dazed Bettie Draper away, and Mary and her baby and an old Dutch woman captive were sold to French traders who resided with the Indians. They could no longer escape as a group. But then, they probably could never have managed it, Mary realized. The children could not walk all the way back to Virginia, and they had no horses, weapons, or food.

Mary and the Dutch woman were trusted and were often sent out without guards to gather nuts for the winter. Mary suggested that the two of them might escape. After they reached Draper's Meadow they could persuade troops from Virginia to come back for Bettie and the children. The old woman agreed, but before they could plan their escape, they were put in canoes and taken farther west to make salt. Again, Mary studied landmarks and counted the rivers they passed. She had to escape now, before they took her even farther west.

One day, when she and the older woman were sent out to the woods, they slipped away, with only a knife, a blanket, and the clothes they wore. Mary's heart ached over leaving her baby behind, but she knew she would be lucky to survive the walk herself, and her baby would surely die on the trek. At least with the Indians the child had a chance at life. Not the life she would have chosen, but a life.

Mary's journey would have been arduous even if she had had a canoe and a weapon. With no tools or weapons, she and the Dutch woman were reduced to eating fruit and nuts. When those gave out with the coming of early winter they subsisted on roots, bugs, worms, tree buds, and bark. Once they stumbled on an abandoned corn field and were able to salvage a few ears. At other times they ate half-rotted pieces of butchered animals they found, scavenging like animals themselves.

Afraid to light a fire for fear of alerting any nearby Indians, they ate everything raw. They suffered debilitating diarrhea, their teeth loosened from malnutrition, and death would almost have been welcome.

Their shoes and clothing fell apart, and the weather grew colder. It was December. Snow fell. Each time they came to a tributary of the Ohio River, they had to walk upstream to a place shallow enough to cross, then go downstream on the other side and continue to the next river. At last, Mary came to the junction with the New River and recognized it.

The Dutch woman, crazed with hunger, attempted to kill Mary, and in their fight the knife was lost. Mary left her and stumbled on alone.

At last, after five months in captivity and six weeks walking, Mary crept into the clearing at Adam Harmon's hut. She was a barely living skeleton, with swollen feet and legs, missing teeth, and white hair—and she was only twenty-three. She had survived a thousand-mile walk. The Harmons happened to be there, completing the last day of harvest. If Mary had arrived one day later, she would have missed them as they were moving into the settlement for safety.

The Dutch woman was rescued and sent along with traders to Pennsylvania. William Ingles and Johnny Draper, who had been searching for their wives, wanted to return to the settlement, but Mary refused to live again at Draper's Meadow with its terrible memories. She moved eastward with William. Two of William's brothers and their families who continued to live on the frontier were later slain by Indians. Mary gradually adjusted to life as an English woman again. She bore three more daughters and another son and lived through two more wars, dying at age eighty-three.

In 1761, Mary's brother, Johnny, ransomed his wife Bettie, who bore him seven more children before she died at age forty-two.

In 1768, Mary and William ransomed their son Thomas for $150.00. Georgie had died soon after Mary's escape, and nothing was ever learned about the fate of their baby daughter. Thomas had difficulty adjusting to life among the English after spending thirteen of his seventeen years with the Indians.

Eventually he married, bought land, and settled down. He was the father of three children when Shawnee Indians attacked in 1782. The fact that he had lived among them didn't help. In a horrible twist of fate, like his father twenty-seven years earlier, Thomas Ingles had to watch helplessly as Indians kidnapped his wife and children and took them away, and he never saw them again.

(An outdoor drama called "The Long Way Home," based on Mary's heroic journey, is performed nightly every summer at the site of Draper's Meadow.)

Getting the Lead Out
·1756·

The lead mines in Wythe County, important in Virginia history for nearly 200 years, were discovered accidentally.

Colonel John Chiswell, who had a mining operation at Fredericksburg, Virginia, was hunting and exploring the area along the New River one day in 1756 when he sensed he was being hunted. Perhaps it was the crackle of a branch that warned him, or maybe it was just a sixth sense. As cautiously as he could, he looked back and caught a glimpse of movement. He was right, and he was in trouble. Indians were pursuing him. Taking a deep breath, he ran as fast as he could and as long as he could, but he knew that Indians could outrace most whites. His only hope for escaping death was to outwit them, and that too was difficult, for most Indians were clever trackers.

Suddenly he came upon a small cave and slipped inside. Miraculously, his pursuers didn't seem to be aware of it. Or would they wait outside until he grew so thirsty and hungry that he came out to be captured?

How long would they wait? How long could he hold out? To pass the time, which seemed interminable, Chiswell began exploring the cave, chipping away bits of rock with his knife. An amateur mineralogist, he realized that the rock contained lead. What a find! But only if he lived to get back to safety.

Chiswell waited out the Indians, escaped, and purchased the land the cave was on. Records show that he recorded five tracts of 400 acres each on the east side of the New River opposite Cripple Creek. The operation became too large for him to handle alone. He formed a partnership with Colonel William Byrd and John Robinson to mine and smelt the lead. The area became known as the Lead Mines.

Much of the lead from their small furnace went toward making bullets that local inhabitants used for hunting and fighting. Other lead was sent to eastern markets. The cave was very profitable, but Chiswell only enjoyed his wealth for a decade.

On a trip back to eastern Virginia, Chiswell was drinking in a tavern in Cumberland County and got into a heated argument with Robert Routledge, another tavern customer. Chiswell drew his sword and killed Routledge, then continued on to his home in Williamsburg, where he hanged himself while awaiting trial for murder. The Lead Mines continued operation under other owners.

When Botetourt County was divided and the county of Fincastle formed, the Lead Mines area was designated as the new county seat. The Lead Mines became a logical gathering place for soldiers on their way to fight because they needed to stock up on lead shot for their muskets. A group met at the mines before marching into the Ohio Territory in 1774 for what became known as the Battle of Point Pleasant.

In 1775, a group of Fincastle men met there to draw up a declaration of their rights, known as the Fincastle Resolutions, a forerunner of the Declaration of Independence.

When the Revolutionary War began, the legislature of Virginia instructed the Committee of Safety for Fincastle County to lease the Lead Mines if the rent were reasonable. If not, they were to seize the mines in the name of the state. The Committee took over the mines and put Charles Lynch of Bedford and a Captain Calloway in charge. They paid rent to Byrd, Robinson, and Chiswell's son.

In the waning days of the Revolution, a group of Loyalists attempted to destroy the Lead Mines, seize supplies in the area, and join Cornwallis's army in the Carolinas. Militia under the direction of Colonel William Preston and Captain William Campbell broke up the group, jailing some and freeing the very young and very old on a promise of good behavior, and hanging some from two white oaks later known as the "Tory Trees." Lynch adopted the latter method of dealing with Loyalists or criminals, and it is from this that the term "lynching" came into being.

After the war, Moses Austin operated the mines while living in a nearby community named for him (Austinville). His son, Stephen Austin, was later known as the Father of Texas.

Late in the 1700s, Thomas Jackson came from Westmoreland, England, to work for the Lead Mine Company as a smith. In 1806 he bought the state's interest in the mines, and in 1809 he began building a tall, monument-like limestone tower to produce lead shot. It was not completed until 1824. Because there was a legal quarrel over ownership of the mine, he built the structure, called Jackson's Ferry Shot Tower, four miles away from the mine itself.

The tower, which is still standing, is 75 feet tall, with a stairway running around the inside of its tapering walls. At the top, molten lead was dropped through a huge circular colander so that it formed a cylindrical shape in its drop down the long shaft into the cold water in a pit below. The tower was used until the 1850s, when a taller one—known as the Shot Shaft—was built at the mine site. This new shaft was located more conveniently and thus became the major shaft of the mine.

During the Civil War Union forces attacked the Lead Mines twice, in 1864 and again in April 1865, only four days before Lee's surrender. In the first raid part of the washing and smelting mill was destroyed. Although the second raid ruined the workings, the mine was back in operation within a year.

In 1863, a Confederate chemist had discovered zinc deposits at the site, just as the lead ore was giving out, so the mine once again became profitable. The mine was purchased in 1901 by the New Jersey Zinc Company.

If Chiswell could have come back in 1956, he would have seen his mine still in operation 200 years after his amazing discovery, producing zinc instead of the lead he had discovered, but producing nevertheless, making it the longest continuously operating mining operation in America.

In 1964, Wythe County citizens raised $5,000.00 to buy the Shot Tower and surrounding land, and the state legislature appropriated money to establish and maintain a public park around the tower.

Virginia's Gentleman Giant
· 1765 ·

On June 23, 1765, two men rowed a boat from a ship to the dock at City Point (now Hopewell) on the Appomattox River, put ashore a dazed little boy, and rowed back to their ship. The ship weighed anchor and moved off downriver.

The child watched for the ship to return. After a while he got up and walked around the dock area, exploring with the curiosity normal for a five year old. He was dressed in a velvet suit and had on well-made shoes with silver buckles monogrammed "PF." People working in the dock area noticed the child, but no one knew who he was. He couldn't' speak English, but when anyone approached, he pointed to himself and said, "Pedro Francisco."

Kind-hearted residents gave him food for the next few days, and someone arranged a safe place for him to sleep in a warehouse near the dock. No one knew where he had come from. Surely someone would come forward to claim such an intelligent, richly dressed little boy. But no one did. Eventually he was admitted to the Prince George County poorhouse as an orphan.

From there he was taken by Judge Anthony Winston to his Buckingham County home, Hunting Tower, to be an indentured servant. The Winstons called the boy Peter Francisco.

Later, when Peter had learned English, he told what he could remember of his life before he was abandoned at City

Point. He had lived in a lovely home near the sea in a faraway place. He described flowers in the garden, a piano, and doting parents. He and his sister had been dressed for a festival and sent out to the garden to play when suddenly men grabbed him and took him to a ship.

Judge Winston was of a prominent family. He was the uncle of Patrick Henry and of the man for whom Winston-Salem, North Carolina, was named. Peter lived with the Winstons for eleven years, working on the farm. He was given food, clothing, and board, but he was never adopted or treated as a member of the family, and he was not educated along with the Winston children.

Peter grew to be a giant: he was 6 feet, 6 inches tall and weighed 260 pounds during a time when the average height for a man was about 5 feet 5 inches. He learned his tasks quickly and worked well, shoeing horses, cutting wood, and tending animals. He was a real asset on the farm.

At Hunting Tower, Peter heard talk of revolution, and he accompanied Judge Winston to Richmond to hear Patrick Henry's fiery speech at St. John's Church in April 1775. Peter listened, enthralled by the dramatic words. He begged to be able to join the militia and fight for his new country, but he was only fourteen and Judge Winston refused permission.

The two returned to Buckingham County, but Peter had not forgotten Henry's speech and the fight for freedom. In December, Judge Winston relented and released Peter, who joined the Continental Army and was sent to New Jersey.

At Brandywine, Pennsylvania, Peter was wounded. The Marquis de Lafayette, also wounded, was hospitalized along with Peter, and the two became lifelong friends. They had much in common. Both were young and foreign born, and both were devoted to the cause of freedom and to General George Washington. Peter returned to action, fought in two more battles, and spent the winter of 1778 at Valley Forge.

Peter was one of twenty commandos chosen by Washington in 1779 to take Stony Point, a strategic fort on the Hudson River. Seventeen were wounded, including Peter Francisco.

When Peter's three-year enlistment ended, he returned to Virginia, but he soon re-enlisted. Legend says that in the thick of the fighting in the Carolinas, when Peter saw that the artillery horses used to pull the cannon had been killed, he picked up the 1,100-pound weapon, shouldered it, and carried it off the field so the British could not capture it.

At Guilford Courthouse, Peter cut his way through the enemy ranks with a huge broadsword ordered especially for him by George Washington. Few men could have lifted it. Peter was wounded by enemy fire and left on the field for dead. He was rescued by a kind Quaker, recovered in six weeks, and walked home to central Virginia.

Peter was famous throughout the new country for his bravery as an ordinary soldier, but he knew that he would have been commissioned as an officer if only he had been able to read and write. He decided that it was not too late to get an education. He attended school with children and made such rapid progress that within three years he was reading the classics. At the same time, he ran a blacksmith shop and established a home in Curdsville, then a town of 300 people (now only a roadside historical marker).

In 1784 Peter married Susannah Anderson and moved to Charlotte County. Stories tell of his prodigious strength: He carried logs 14 feet long and more than a foot in diameter to build his house. County records for the next decade show Peter buying and selling land and livestock and serving on juries. In 1790 Susannah died, leaving him with two small children.

On a visit to his mother-in-law's house, Peter fell in love with Susannah's cousin, Catherine Brooke, and soon married her. The couple had four children. The popular Franciscos entertained and were entertained throughout the state. Several writers mentioned Peter's excellent singing voice, and two songs that he composed still exist.

Out of consideration for his friends' furniture, Peter had twelve giant chairs made and gave one to each of twelve friends for his use when he visited.

Although Peter was a hero for his service in the Revolutionary War, his only reward was $50.00 in compensation for the loss of his horse during battle. In 1818 he was granted a pension of $8.00 per month. In the following year a ship built in Richmond was named for him; the *Peter Francisco* sank in 1823.

A highlight of Peter's later years was a visit to America by the Marquis de Lafayette in 1824. Peter attended a ball in honor of Lafayette in Petersburg, near the site where he had been abandoned as a child. The two friends, now old men, enjoyed reminiscing about the Revolution.

Peter Francisco spent his last three years as sergeant at arms to the Virginia legislature. At his death in 1831 both the Senate and the House of Delegates were adjourned in his honor. He was given a full military funeral, attended by the governor and Virginia's elected officials. He was honored by his adopted country but died not knowing the truth about his real home and family.

In 1960, nearly two centuries after Peter's arrival in America, the story of his background was discovered. Researchers found a birth certificate in the Azores, Atlantic island that belonged to Portugal, for Pedro Francisco, born in 1760. He would have been five years old when he was put ashore in Virginia. His father, a prominent nobleman, had been on bad terms with the king, who secretly ordered the death of one of Francisco's children. The disappearance of the boy was also recorded in Portuguese court documents. Peter Francisco's mystery was at last solved.

A Midnight Ride
· 1781 ·

The Revolutionary War was in its final months in June 1781, although neither side realized it. British General Lord Charles Cornwallis had been defeated at Cowpens in the Carolinas and now invaded Virginia, the largest colony. Many of Virginia's troops were fighting elsewhere, and General Washington's forces were tied down in New York. Virginia was virtually unprotected.

Just months before, Benedict Arnold had sailed up the James River from Portsmouth to Richmond and demanded all the tobacco stored there. When Thomas Jefferson, then governor of Virginia, refused, Arnold torched the public buildings and military supplies.

The capital had been transferred to Richmond from Williamsburg only the year before because Williamsburg, on a peninsula between two rivers, was considered too exposed to invasion. Now Richmond was also unsafe. Jefferson moved the colony's government from Richmond to Charlottesville.

Cornwallis, who had marched as far north as Hanover County, north of Richmond, gave a special mission to Banastre Tarleton, known as "Butcher Tarleton" for his treatment of colonial troops and civilians in the Carolinas and also known as "The Hunting Leopard." Tarleton was to surprise, take, or disperse the members of the legislature and to capture Governor Jefferson. Actually, Jefferson was no longer governor by the time Tarleton began his march; his term had expired June 1. But he was known throughout the colonies as the main author of the Declaration of Independence, and he could possibly be held for ransom. In addition, the legislature included three other signers of the Declaration of Independence and Patrick Henry, also a well-known rebel. They were worth the capture.

Tarleton set off with 180 cavalry and seventy mounted infantrymen. By the late evening of June 3 they had reached Cuckoo Tavern in Louisa County. Tarleton's plan was foiled by the quick thinking and hard riding of Captain John Jouett, a member of the Virginia militia.

Jouett was in the tavern having ale when Tarleton's troops approached. Guessing their destination was not difficult. As unobtrusively as possible, Jouett set down his tankard and slipped outside. He leaped onto his horse and rode toward Charlottesville to warn the legislators. He had an advantage: He knew the backroads and shortcuts that Tarleton didn't know. Jouett followed Three-Chopt Road, while Tarleton continued on the longer Louisa Road. Moreover, Tarleton was unaware of Jouett; or if he knew, he didn't care. He was in command of battle-hardened British soldiers, the best in the world, and he knew that Jefferson and the government were unprotected. The capture would be easy.

While Jouett rode furiously toward Charlottesville, helped by a full moon to light his way, Tarleton's troops stopped for a three-hour rest. Then they saddled up, regrouped, and were on their way when they overtook twelve wagons loaded with clothing for the American armies in the South. Tarleton stopped the wagons, examined the cargo, and set it all ablaze. The British had no need of additional clothing, but the threadbare American soldiers did. This destruction took time and further delayed Tarleton's journey to Charlottesville.

The British delayed yet again close to Charlottesville when they captured several Virginians from the Tidewater area who had fled upcountry for safety. Some were questioned and released as harmless; others were taken prisoner and had to be guarded. All this took more time.

Jouett, meanwhile, unaware of Tarleton's leisurely journey, had spurred on his horse constantly, pushing the lathered animal to complete the 40-mile ride just as the sun came up. He reached Charlottesville on his sweating, panting horse hours ahead of Tarleton's raiders. He went first to Jefferson's home, Monticello, which is on a hilltop outside the city, to warn Jefferson.

Upon receiving the warning, the speaker of the General Assembly, who was having breakfast with Jefferson, rose from the table and rode immediately to Charlottesville to round up the members of the government. They met quickly and adjourned, agreeing to convene again in Staunton, 40 miles farther west, on June 7. Most of the legislators escaped, but a few were taken prisoner, along with some soldiers who attempted to protect the public stores of Charlottesville.

Tarleton had sent ahead one of his raiders with instructions to guard Monticello and leave the house intact. Tarleton himself was detained at Castle Hill by the Walker family, friends of Jefferson. The Walkers kept offering Tarleton one delicious breakfast dish after another to give Jefferson and the legislators extra time to get away.

Jefferson finished his breakfast, packed up his papers and personal belongings, and left Monticello with his family just minutes before one of Tarleton's raiders came up the other side of the hill. The raider remained at Monticello for eighteen hours before rejoining his commander.

Tarleton spared Monticello, but he took revenge on another of Jefferson's properties, Elk Hill, near Richmond. All the livestock and the tobacco crop were stolen. Tarleton then ordered the buildings and even the fences burned, leaving the place a wasteland.

In appreciation of Jouett's service, the Virginia legislature passed a resolution granting him an "elegant sword and pair of pistols as a memorial of the high sense which the General Assembly entertain for his activity and enterprise." He received the pistols in 1783, but not until twenty years later was the sword presented by Governor James Monroe.

Jouett moved to Kentucky and served in its legislature.

Tarleton rejoined Cornwallis and, after the war, returned to England. Jefferson went on to become secretary of state and then third president of the United States.

Victory, with Help from Our Friends

·1781·

The American Revolution had dragged on for six years after that "shot heard 'round the world" at Lexington. General George Washington had eluded the British time after time, escaping to fight again. His troops had endured hardship, cold, and hunger. Some had died, some had deserted, and some had drifted away when their enlistments were up. Many had given up hope of an American victory. After all, the British army was the biggest and best in the world. The ragtag American army was poorly trained, poorly equipped, and often not paid.

In the late summer of 1781 Washington saw a chance to win independence, possibly his final chance. Sometimes things happen as if by fate, and this seemed to be one of those times. Events were playing into his hands.

Early in 1781 British General Lord Charles Cornwallis had marched north to Virginia from the conquered Carolinas. Benedict Arnold had led an army of Loyalists that burned Richmond and laid waste to outlying plantations before heading north to Connecticut. Banastre Tarleton and Lieutenant Colonel John Graves Simcoe were also in Virginia. Opposing them were General Baron von Steuben, General "Mad" Anthony Wayne, and French General Marquis de Lafayette.

After several forays to Richmond and beyond, Cornwallis set up an encampment on the banks of the York River at Yorktown. His entire army was in Yorktown by August 22. August is often an unpleasant time in Virginia, especially in the low-lying Tidewater area. The British in heavy woolen uniforms had to contend with heat, humidity, and, at night, mosquitoes.

Cornwallis could defend his position because Yorktown is a peninsula, but Washington realized that Cornwallis also could be blocked in, if the French fleet could hold off the British and prevent the resupplying of Cornwallis's troops.

A large French army under the General Comte de Rochambeau had arrived in Rhode Island with instructions to cooperate with Washington. The two generals met and planned an attack on New York, to be supported by the French fleet under Admiral François Joseph Paul DeGrasse. Word arrived that the fleet would arrive in America in July or August. Washington sent a message suggesting that the fleet come to New York, stopping off at Chesapeake Bay on the way.

Washington considered three plans: an attack on New York, a campaign in Virginia, or a siege of Charleston. Word arrived that DeGrasse would leave the West Indies on August 13 and would leave the American coast on October 15. Whatever Washington did had to be done during that two-month period. The British outnumbered the allies in New York, but in combination with other American armies in Virginia, Washington would command a superior force. Charleston was too far away to reach in time. Thus Virginia was chosen.

To mislead the British, Washington wrote General Lafayette about plans to attack New York, intending for the letter to fall into British hands. It did, and while the British maintained troop strength in New York, Washington and Rochambeau slipped away and marched south.

The British admiral Thomas Graves in the West Indies heard rumors of DeGrasse's move to America but felt confident he would only take a small portion of the French fleet. Surely the French would not expose their West Indian islands to

British attack. By the time Graves realized that the entire fleet was gone, it was too late for pursuit.

On August 28, the British in New York discovered that eight French ships that had been at Newport, Rhode Island, had sailed south to the Chesapeake. Eighteen British ships sailed to intercept them. When they reached the coast of Virginia between capes Henry and Charles, however, they discovered not the eight ships they had been warned about but DeGrasse's entire fleet of twenty-four ships.

For five days the two fleets fought, without a decisive victory for either. On the fifth day the eight French ships from Rhode Island arrived and slipped into Chesapeake Bay. The British withdrew, returning to New York for repairs.

British General Henry Clinton realized that Cornwallis needed reinforcements. He wrote to Cornwallis to say that he would set sail as soon as the convoy was ready, and he loaded 7,000 troops onto British ships. However, the British fleet had been so badly damaged in the scuffle with the French ships that it was six weeks before the ships were able to sail again, and by that time the fight in Virginia was over.

Now isolated from the rest of the British army, and with his retreat blocked by the French fleet, Cornwallis, with his 5,000 troops, prepared his defenses. To the west and south of Yorktown the land was marshy. To the north was the river. On the east, in hilly terrain, Cornwallis had built a stockade with an earthen parapet and a ring of redoubts and batteries. Considering his situation, the defenses were excellent. But nothing could save him from defeat.

Washington, Rochambeau, and Lafayette closed in, bringing with them siege guns from the French fleet. First the outer defenses fell, then the inner. On the night of October 14, the Americans and French stormed the redoubts.

Cornwallis made a final effort to save the situation, attempting to ferry his troops across the York River to Gloucester Point during the night of October 16. From there he could march north to Philadelphia. However, circumstances defeated him. A sudden storm scattered his boats and swamped some of them. He decided to surrender.

The next morning Cornwallis wrote Washington asking for an armistice. Washington, fearing rightly that Clinton was on his way from New York, granted only a two hour ceasefire, which he later extended to half a day. Terms were agreed upon, and the surrender was signed on October 19, 1781. Although the British were still in control of Charleston, Savannah, and New York, the war was effectively over.

Although Washington's strategy and determination were important, the battle would not have been won without the French fleet. The "indecisive battle" in the capes of Chesapeake Bay proved very decisive a month later at Yorktown.

Washington resigned as commander of the American forces in December 1782. Cornwallis returned to England and became governor general of India, winning for Britain a territory as large as that he had lost in America. The French had gotten revenge on the British for past wars and had earned the immense gratitude of the Americans, but that was their only gain. They incurred a heavy debt during the American Revolution that contributed to their own revolution a few years later.

Yorktown, Virginia, is a small, quiet town today. The only indications of its past importance are the Victory Monument, the visitors' center, and the cannons by the river pointing at the earthworks where an empire was lost and won.

The Bizarre
Randolphs
· 1792 ·

As carriages full of Randolphs rolled toward Glentivar Plantation in Cumberland County on September 30, 1792, only two of the group might have guessed that a scandal was about to erupt that would touch the highest-ranking Virginians.

The wealthy, prolific Randolphs had a habit of marrying their cousins and marrying young, and this group was no exception. Judith Randolph, then nineteen, was married to her cousin, Richard Randolph, who was three years older. They were living at nearby Bizarre Plantation with their four-month-old son and Judith's sister, Ann Cary Randolph, called Nancy. Nancy, a pretty, vivacious seventeen year old, had been engaged to Richard's brother, Theodorick, who had died of tuberculosis at Bizarre on February 14. A third brother, John Randolph, had a love-hate relationship with Nancy. According to Nancy, he made romantic advances to her and when she spurned him, he turned vengeful.

Ever since Theodorick's death, Nancy had been depressed and sometimes hysterical. On that September night, she said at dinner that she felt ill, so she left the table and went upstairs to bed. Some guests at Glentivar heard her screaming in the night, then heard someone go downstairs and outside. The next morning there were bloodstains on Nancy's bed linens, but no hostess would confront a female guest over such a matter.

Nothing was said about the events of the night, and for the remainder of the visit all seemed well.

Before the end of the month, however, John Randolph was told by another cousin that the slaves at Glentivar had found a dead white baby in a pile of shingles behind the plantation house. Gossip spread that the baby was Nancy's, fathered by Richard, her sister's husband, and that he had killed the newborn. Richard threatened a lawsuit for slander and planned to take Judith and Nancy away for the summer while the lawsuit was being heard, but events took another turn. By April, Richard was in jail, charged with murdering the baby. Nancy, also charged, was in the custody of her lawyers.

The courthouse at Cumberland was packed for the trial. After all, the defendants were from one of the most socially prominent, powerful families in Virginia. So were the lawyers. John Marshall, a Randolph cousin, who later became a chief justice of the Supreme Court, defended Richard and Nancy, aided by Patrick Henry. Attending the trial was Martha Jefferson Randolph, whose husband was brother to Nancy and Judith.

Witnesses said that Richard Randolph had gone up and down the stairs that strange night at Glentivar, but Judith testified that the only door to Nancy's room was beside her bed, and that Richard had remained at her side all night and had certainly not gone to Nancy.

One witness described looking through a keyhole at Nancy during the summer and suspecting a pregnancy. The lawyers made much fun of her snooping at keyholes, and her testimony was somewhat discredited.

There was no adequate description of the baby found in the shingle pile because the slaves who had discovered the body could not testify under Virginia law. It was impossible to determine if it had been a fetus or a full-term baby. In the latter case, the baby could have been Theodorick's.

Eventually, charges against Richard and Nancy were dropped, which was good for the lawyers' reputations, but Richard's and

Nancy's reputations had been ruined by the lawsuit. Worse, Nancy had no home except at Bizarre with Richard and Judith. John Randolph was also living there, having sold his plantation at Richard's suggestion.

In June 1796, John was in Petersburg when he became ill with what he described as a "bilious fever." Richard visited him there and on his return to Bizarre became ill himself and died. John accused Nancy of poisoning Richard, but it is likely that Richard died of the illness John had.

Fortunately for Nancy, an unexpected visitor had been at Bizarre and was a reliable witness. Benjamin Latrobe, who later designed the United States Capitol, was in 1796 an itinerant architect and general handyman. He lost his way in a storm and took refuge at Bizarre. He later described Richard's illness and stated that a doctor was attending him.

Richard's will freed the Bizarre Plantation slaves. Judith carried out her husband's wishes and continued to run the plantation with hired labor. Nancy stayed on, and later said that she was treated like a servant, except that she was not paid and was allowed to sit at the family table. Judith, grieving for her husband and worried over finances, began to quarrel with Nancy, and John accused Nancy of having an affair with one of the slaves.

Eventually, Nancy fled from Bizarre and made lengthy visits to various family plantations. She had eleven siblings besides Judith, but because of her reputation she was not the most welcome of visitors. Destitute, she moved to Richmond and lived in a rented room. John Randolph would not relent in his attacks on her. He claimed she supported herself in Richmond as a prostitute.

At age thirty-one, unmarried and penniless, Nancy taught briefly at a Connecticut school and then moved to New York. In New York, Nancy was visited by the wealthy and worldly Gouverneur Morris, former minister to France, who had known her as a child at Tuckahoe Plantation in Virginia. He needed a housekeeper, he said, a "gentlewoman in reduced circum-stances" who could control the servants, and she would be ad-mirably suited. Nancy accepted the position.

Morris, then in his fifties, had never married, and his nieces and nephews counted on inheriting his fortune. To their shock and outrage, however, Morris married Nancy Randolph on Christmas Day in 1809. Ever one to criticize, John Randolph (now calling himself John Randolph of Roanoke) wrote a long diatribe against Nancy and sent it to her husband. To his credit, Morris believed none of it and indeed wrote to a friend how happily married he was and what an intelligent and affection-ate wife Nancy was.

The Randolph and Morris kin were all surprised when Gouverneur and Nancy became the parents of a son, Gou-verneur Jr., in February 1813.

Morris died in 1816 of natural causes, and in his will he made Nancy both guardian and trustee of his fortune and of their son. She was for the first time in her life financially secure, one of the few Randolphs to be free of money worries. Cousins who had declined to invite her for a visit now wrote offering family support in her time of trouble.

Nancy, however, had learned by necessity to look after herself and had no need of family support. She was a capable manager of the Morris money and was pleased when her son married a Randolph first cousin from Virginia.

Her sister Judith had also died in 1816, several months be-fore Morris. Bizarre had burned down, and Judith spent her last years in a house in Farmville.

John Randolph of Roanoke never married. The only woman he proposed to married his cousin, Peyton Randolph. John served nearly three decades in Congress and lived alone at Roanoke Plantation, raising hunting dogs and race horses.

Gabriel's Insurrection
• 1800 •

N at Turner's Rebellion is famous, but few outside Virginia have heard of Gabriel's Insurrection, or Gabriel's Conspiracy. Turner and his followers slew sixty whites in a small area. What Gabriel Prosser planned was mass killing and takeover of the entire state of Virginia. He almost succeeded.

After the American Revolution, slaves hoped to obtain their freedom, especially since some of them had fought alongside their owners for freedom from Great Britain. For a few years, their conditions improved. They were punished less and given more freedom to travel, worship, have social gatherings, and learn.

Then news spread to Virginia about a slave rebellion in Haiti. Virginia's slaves began to wonder if they could fight for their own freedom and bring down a government, as slaves just like themselves had done in Haiti. Whites wondered too, especially after a shipload of French refugees from Haiti arrived in Norfolk and some were sheltered in the Richmond area. Seeing others like themselves who had barely escaped slaughter, the plantation owners worried and looked for conspiracies.

Reports came to Richmond of unusual meetings among slaves in Cumberland, Mathews, and Warwick Counties, and in Yorktown, Petersburg, and Portsmouth in 1793. State militia were armed and slave owners went on the alert. But nothing happened. For seven years there was an uneasy calm in Virginia, until Gabriel Prosser organized his rebellion.

Gabriel was a slave living at Thomas Prosser's Brookfield Plantation in Henrico County, along with his brothers, Solomon and Martin. Only twenty-four years old, Gabriel was an extremely competent leader, managing to organize a scheme that covered a wide area and included hundreds, if not thousands, of blacks, both slave and free. So carefully was it planned that no word of it leaked out until a few hours before the massacre was to begin.

For weeks, blacks who were fishing, loading boats, preaching sermons, or working in the fields spread the message. Evening meetings were held, made possible by the new freedom slaves had to attend church or social gatherings.

No records were kept on how many blacks were involved. Indeed, most insurrectionists could not read or write. Gabriel claimed that 10,000 were ready to revolt. Gabriel's second-in-command, a huge slave named Jack Bowler, attempted to take over the leadership, but Gabriel put the decision to a vote of his followers and won.

The insurrectionists did more than just talk; they made weapons. Many of the slaves involved were plantation blacksmiths, which made it easy for them to sharpen farm implements into lethal weapons or to fashion knives from bits of scrap metal. They also made bows and arrows and collected any stout tree branch or rock that could be used to club a victim. They stole muskets, bullets, and powder.

The plan was to start a fire in a warehouse on the Richmond waterfront during the night of August 30. When the whites rushed to fight the fire, slaves from outside the city would come in and slaughter the exhausted firefighters. Next, the insurrectionists planned to seize the treasury, kidnap Governor James Monroe, open the penitentiary, and release all the prisoners to join the uprising.

All slaveowners and their wives and children would be killed, starting with Gabriel's owner, Thomas Prosser. Some conspirators later testified that Gabriel planned to spare

Methodists, Quakers, and French colonists. Once the city had been seized and its leading citizens killed, Gabriel was certain slaves from the outlying areas would come into Richmond to join his rebellion. It would spread throughout the state.

Whites in Richmond felt a vague uneasiness throughout August. Things just didn't seem right, but there was no specific threat they could respond to. Then on Saturday, August 30, slaves who usually went into Richmond to enjoy themselves stayed put or headed north to Gabriel's set meeting place.

That day, two slaves fearfully approached their owner, Mosby Sheppard, on his plantation in Henrico County and told him about the plot. Sheppard believed them and hastened to inform Governor Monroe. The governor called up the militia and had them patrol the streets and roads, the penitentiary, and other public buildings, but the warning would have come too late if nature had not intervened.

That afternoon, a terrifying storm struck the Richmond area. Trees were downed and roads and streams were flooded, making travel all but impossible. Because of the storm, Gabriel Prosser postponed his attack until the following night, but by then it was too late. The government was in control of events. Gabriel's plan for a massacre was abandoned, and the leaders of the insurrection fled.

Most were captured quickly, although Jack Bowler eluded the militia for two weeks and Gabriel Prosser for nearly a month. Gabriel hid out in the lowlands along the James River and hailed a passing ship, which picked him up. Two slaves onboard recognized him and informed the captain. A Methodist and an antislavery advocate, the captain did nothing, although there was a reward for Gabriel's capture. When the ship docked in Norfolk, the two slaves got word to the sheriff, and Gabriel was arrested.

Governor Monroe urged calm and told the legislature that Virginia must make certain the trials of the insurrectionists were conducted fairly. Many of the accused revealed the details of the plot, but Gabriel himself refused to testify. He was found guilty and was hanged, along with about twenty-four others. The owners of those slaves put to death were compensated by the state government.

Many of the conspirators were acquitted and others were granted clemency, sometimes at the request of the very people they had planned to kill, on condition of being taken out of the state.

The breakup of this particular conspiracy did not end slave uprisings. Attempts at insurrection were discovered in Virginia and North Carolina in 1801, 1802, 1808, 1809, and 1813, sometimes with sympathetic whites participating along with blacks. None was as extensive as Gabriel Prosser's planned insurrection, and none resulted in great loss of life until Nat Turner's Rebellion in 1831.

A Traitor on Trial
· 1807 ·

The trial of Aaron Burr was the biggest social occasion Richmond had seen in years and a political event as well. It pitted President Thomas Jefferson against his political rival and cousin, John Marshall, chief justice of the Supreme Court, as well as against Burr, former vice president.

Burr and Jefferson's rivalry began in 1800, when both wanted to become president. Although Burr had run for vice president, electors made no distinction between the two offices and there was no clear winner of the presidency, so the vote went to the House of Representatives, where Jefferson won on the thirty-sixth ballot, by a single vote. Burr became vice president. Jefferson stripped Burr of jobs and benefits that should have been his to give out, and in 1804 Jefferson chose George Clinton, Burr's chief rival in New York State, to be his vice president.

In 1803, the United States bought the vast Louisiana Territory. While he was still vice president, Burr went to the British minister in Washington and offered to break away the western United States in return for £110,000 (pounds sterling) and the support of the British fleet on the Mississippi River. The British declined, but Burr went ahead with this treasonous plans anyway.

In 1804, Alexander Hamilton publicly insulted Burr, who responded by challenging Hamilton to a duel. The duel was held in New Jersey. The two men exchanged shots and Hamilton fell, mortally wounded. Some people believed Burr was guilty of murder.

By 1806 Burr had organized a group to take over the Louisiana Purchase. That group included General James Wilkerson, who had earlier attempted treason with Spain against the United States.

Apparently President Jefferson knew of the conspiracy but did nothing about it for ten months. Wilkerson himself then warned Jefferson that Burr was attempting to set up a kingdom in the west and to make himself its king. At that point President Jefferson had Burr arrested and brought to Richmond for trial.

Burr's preliminary hearing was held at a Richmond tavern, and he was granted bail. His aristocratic manner so impressed two Richmond men that they signed his bond for $5,000.00 and gave him $1,000.00 to buy suitable clothing to replace his shabby attire. The following day Justice Marshall set May 22 as the day Burr's case would be presented to the grand jury.

Burr, free to move about the city, was popular with Richmonders. Some of the most prominent citizens vied to entertain the handsome, charming New Yorker. One member of Burr's defense team, attorney John Wickham, even gave a dinner for Burr that John Marshall attended. This would now be considered an conflict of interest, and even then it drew criticism as showing favoritism toward the defendant.

But Jefferson was equally prejudiced. Instead of leaving the conduct of the trial up to the prosecutor, Jefferson tried to direct the trial himself, sending written evidence and suggestions for obtaining a conviction. He offered blanket pardons to any Burr associates who would testify against Burr and even offered a commission in the United States Navy to a French adventurer if he would testify for the government.

Burr's defense team included the highly praised lawyer Benjamin Botts; Edmund Randolf, former attorney general of the United States and also a cousin of Jefferson; and four other prominent attorneys. Marshall appointed as foreman of the grand jury John Randolph of Roanoke, yet another cousin of Marshall and Jefferson who disliked Jefferson. However, he also disliked Aaron Burr. The grand jury members read like a veritable "who's who" of Virginia, but it included more Republicans—members of Jefferson's party—than Federalists, whom Marshall supported.

The prosecution's chief witness was Wilkerson, who narrowly missed being indicted for treason himself. The incriminating cipher letter that he claimed Burr had written had been altered. Still, the grand jury found that there was enough evidence against Burr to hold him for trial.

After Burr was indicted, he spent only two nights in the local jail. Released, he lived for some time under guard in a private home in Richmond before being given a suite of rooms in the newly built penitentiary. He was quite comfortable and was treated well, he wrote his daughter. He received a stream of visitors, some of whom brought him words of encouragement as well as more practical things: fruits and berries, butter and cream, toilet articles, and ice, a very important gift in Richmond's sweltering summer heat.

The trial, held in the Capitol, attracted throngs of spectators. All hotels and boarding houses were booked for the event. People rented out rooms in their home, and visitors unable to find lodging camped out in tents or in the open along the river. They arrived by carriage, wagons, and boats, on horseback, and on foot, families and single people. Frontiersmen and farmers came in buckskin; wealthier people wore their best silks and velvets to attend the trial. They packed the Capitol and stood on the lawn outside. Burr was the celebrity of the day, and they wanted to get a look at him and hear what was said. Most thought he was clearly guilty and should hang for his crime.

The trial itself, which finally began on August 2, 1807, attracted its own share of celebrities and journalists. Among those attending was General Andrew Jackson, who had entertained Burr at The Hermitage, his home in Tennessee. Jackson called the trial political persecution. Covering the trial for New

York newspapers was young Washington Irving, later to become famous as a novelist. He wrote articles favorable to Burr and praised Richmond's hospitality.

Event though Burr was probably guilty of trying to set up a foreign government in the west, Justice Marshall made it almost impossible for the jury to convict him of treason. Treason, he said, must be an overt act, not merely a plan. Moreover, each act must be witnessed by two persons who must then testify.

The prosecution was dumfounded. How could they produce two witnesses to each conversation? And because no attack had actually happened, no coup actually carried out, there had been no overt act to witness. The prosecution had planned lengthy presentation of witnesses to Burr's intentions, but that was now useless. They ended the trial quickly.

It took the jury only twenty-five minutes to reach a verdict. They declared that Burr had not been proven guilty by the evidence presented. Burr objected that the statement was not a clear acquittal. Marshall then directed that the record show "not guilty."

After the trial was over, Burr left the United States and lived in Europe. He later returned to New York and practiced as an attorney.

The Richmond
Theater Fire
· 1811 ·

From his blacksmith shop, Gilbert Hunt, a slave, may have watched enviously as crowds of well-dressed people passed on their way to Richmond's new theater on Shockhoe Hill the day after Christmas in 1811. But before the evening was over, many of those people would be dead, and many of the survivors would owe their lives to Hunt.

Christmas was a festive season in Virginia, a time of weddings, feasts, lengthy visits to relatives, and entertainment, such as the December 26 theatrical performances. First on the playbill was a French comedy, *The Father, or Family Feuds,* by Diderot, followed by a musical interlude. The climax of the program was a brand new melodrama, *Raymond and Agnes, or The Bleeding Nun.* The blood-and-thunder melodrama was being presented for the first time in Richmond, and the audience was eagerly awaiting it.

In the audience was the newly elected governor of Virginia, George W. Smith, accompanied by a lovely young lady. The 650 persons attending also included former U.S. Senator Abraham Venable, then president of the Bank of Virginia; Benjamin Botts, the brilliant attorney who had defended Aaron Burr, and Mrs. Botts; Lieutenant James Gibbon, a veteran of the fighting in the Mediterranean against the Barbary pirates, resplendent in his military uniform, and his sweetheart, Sally

Conyers; and many other prominent Richmond citizens, as well as laborers and servants.

The wealthier playgoers entered by the main door and went up the winding stairway to one of the three levels of box seats. Here they could see the play and be seen and admired by others. The cheaper seats were even higher up but were reached by an outside staircase, a fact that saved many lives.

All went well until the main feature. The first scene, lit by a candle-filled chandelier, ended with Raymond and Agnes escaping from robbers. As the curtain fell, the audience applauded and the stagehands began to prepare for the second act. The backdrop of the first act was raised, along with the still-lighted chandelier. The backdrop for the next scene, a painting of a castle, was lowered. The stagehand raising the chandelier hesitated, but someone from below told him to haul it up. He kept pulling, bringing it closer to the very flammable draperies and oil painted scenery. Finally the stage manager ordered that the candles be extinguished. As the stagehand lowered the chandelier, the rope holding it became tangled. Instead of descending smoothly, the chandelier began swinging back and forth, and in an instant it had set fire to the scenery.

The curtain rose for the second scene and the leading actor began speaking, unaware of frantic efforts to put out the fire backstage. But it was already too late. Nearly everything in the building was combustible: costumes, scenery, props, and the building and boxes themselves. As bits of burned scenery began to drift down onto the stage, the actor realized what was happening, cut short his lines, and cried out, "The house is on fire!"

The terrified audience pushed for the exits. Those in the pit on the main floor managed to escape out to the street, but playgoers in the boxes had to come out into narrow corridors and make their way to the single staircase. A few in the lower tier of boxes risked broken bones, jumping onto the stage and then into the pit to escape.

Dense black smoke filled the theater, and the screams of the doomed tore the air as their clothing caught fire. Some suffocated from the smoke, others were crushed by the mad push onto the stairway to the solitary exit, and still others jumped to their death or were crushed by others jumping after them.

There were scenes of heroism and self-sacrifice. Benjamin Botts, the attorney, managed to reach safety but then went back to find his wife, and both were burned to death. Governor Smith also got to the outside door but turned back gallantly to save the young woman he had brought to the theater, and he perished with her. Miss Conyers fainted and Lieutenant Gibbon and a friend were carrying her out when Gibbon told his friend to go ahead, he could carry Sally by himself, but the lovers didn't make it. They were burned so badly that their bodies could only be identified by the buttons on his uniform and a necklace she was wearing.

The middle section of the stairway broke under the weight of the crowd, crushing those underneath. Then the upper section tore away, sending more victims plummeting on top of those who had already fallen. Before they could escape, the flames reached them.

Outside, tolling fire bells brought people running from all directions. Many had loved ones who had gone to the theater, and they could only watch helplessly as flames consumed the building.

As Gilbert Hunt ran toward the fire, he begged a neighbor for a bed and mattress to catch those who would jump. He was refused. Nevertheless, he went to help. Dr. James McCaw was at a window trying to help terrified ladies down. Hunt, his arms powerful and muscular from hammering iron, caught the women as Dr. McCaw lowered them to the ground. Together, they saved about a dozen women.

Hunt saw that a burning wall was about to collapse and urged McCaw to jump and save himself. At the last possible moment the doctor jumped and lay so still that Hunt thought the brave man was dead. Then McCaw screamed in pain, and Hunt carried him to safety before the burning timbers could fall on him.

By morning the fire had burned itself out. All that remained were smoldering timbers and charred bodies. Men went in with rakes and shovels, uncovering the grisly remains of those who had been Richmond's leaders and workers. Seventy-six had died outright in the burning building and four more died later of injuries and burns. The Richmond Enquirer published a casualty list two days later. Among the dead were Pages, Nelsons, and Braxtons, families whose ancestors had founded the nation. Also listed were some whose names were followed by "a youth," "a stranger," and "a woman of color, free."

Because of the impossibility of separating and removing the remains, they were all buried in a common grave three days later, on the site of theater. Stores in Richmond were shuttered for two days and theaters throughout the nation closed for periods of mourning. Sermons were preached against theatergoing and dancing, and public shows were prohibited in Richmond for four months.

Episcopalians built a church, Monumental Church, on the site of the theater in memory of those who died. A plaque was also erected in recognition of Gilbert Hunt, a man who could not attend the theater but helped save those who did.

The Unhappy Soldier
·1829·

Sergeant Major Perry paced along the top of the five-sided wall enclosing Fort Monroe, Virginia. He had just been promoted to the highest rank an enlisted man could have, less than two years after his enlistment in May 1827. He had enlisted on a whim, in a desperate effort to escape debt and unhappiness, but his enlistment hadn't solved anything. He longed to leave the army and live the gentlemanly life to which he was accustomed.

After all, he was no ordinary soldier. He was the adopted son of one of the wealthiest merchants in Richmond, not that his foster father had ever been generous with him. At least not in the last three years.

It had been different when he was a child. His foster father had seemed proud of him then, bragging about the little boy's excellent memory and ability to recite poetry. The soldier remembered being dressed up in a velvet suit and allowed to entertain guests when his family stayed at White Sulphur Springs, even being allowed to give toasts to the ladies and take a sip of wine. Then, at age eight, he'd gone with his foster father, his adored foster mother, Frances, and her sister, Nancy, to England for five years. There he'd been enrolled in an English school for boys, where he studied French, Latin, mathematics, and literature. The schoolmasters thought he was too indulged and spoiled by his foster father. They should see him now!

Sergeant Major Perry realized that his situation could be much worse. He could have been sent to the frontier instead of to the fort overlooking Hampton Roads harbor, not far from Richmond. How he longed to be in Richmond, to see his foster mother. She was ill, but he couldn't visit her.

A chilly wind blew off Chesapeake Bay, cutting through the fabric of his uniform. How could he endure losing his foster mother? His own mother had died giving birth to his sister, and Jane, the mother of his best friend and a person to whom he'd been close, had died too.

He disliked the fort. A moat enclosed its walls; one could only enter or leave the fort by a narrow bridge. Inside the fort were a series of dungeonlike rooms with low, curved ceilings and tiny, deepset windows. It had been designed to protect the harbor after the disastrous beating the American Navy took in the bay and at sea during the War of 1812. The fort was sturdy and well-planned but gloomy, and Perry needed cheering up.

He stared down into the depths of the moat, its dark, glassy surface mirroring his sadness. He had written poems about love and death and had even arranged to have a group of them published, but poetry was no way to earn a living. Neither was being an enlisted man. The pay was too low to support his tastes, and he had climbed up the ranks as far as he could get. Perhaps his foster father would pay a substitute to take his place and secure an appointment for him at West Point. Perry had already written him, begging for this support, but the answer was, "I feel you should stay where you are."

He crumpled up his foster father's latest letter and dropped it into the water. They had fought ever since he'd turned fifteen. He'd gone off to the University of Virginia with high hopes and precious little else. His father saw to that. How could he have been expected to pay his fees and expenses with no money?

The University of Virginia, founded by Thomas Jefferson, was different from America's other colleges, which all had religious support and religious programs. At the university there was no need to attend the Episcopal church or any other, and Perry hadn't. College rules forbade the ownership of horses, dogs, servants, guns, tobacco, wine, and liquor, but the rules were widely ignored.

He'd tried gambling to make up the difference between the $100.00 his father had given him and the cost of a year in Charlottesville, $150.00 at a minimum. Most students spent $500.00. With no experience in gambling, he'd lost badly at cards and suspected he had been cheated.

He'd gotten into fights and held his own and was drunk more than he should have been. It seemed that alcohol affected him more quickly than it did others: A single drink could make him roaring drunk, almost insane.

Still, he'd done well academically. He'd completed two years at the university, although only one-quarter of students who enrolled managed to stay for two years.

But debt caught up with Perry. His foster father had paid off some of his debts and brought him home to Richmond to work as an unpaid clerk in the family business. Here he learned to write business letters and do financial accounting, but he hated business. At the same time, the young woman he'd fallen in love with had become engaged to someone else.

At that point Perry had left Richmond and taken a ship to Boston, where he worked as a warehouse clerk on the waterfront and then as a newspaper reporter. But the pay was too low to live on, so he had joined the army for five years, swearing that he was twenty-one years old, although he was only eighteen. He gave his name as Edgar Perry. At least he would have security and a roof over his head for five years, he thought.

Edgar Perry hated the army but did well nevertheless. His superior officers recognized his ability and assigned him the job of company clerk at $5.00 a month. He made out the payroll and master rolls, wrote letters, and acted as a messenger.

After six months in Boston, during which he had a forty-page booklet of his poetry published, he was sent to Charleston, South Carolina, and then to Fort Monroe.

Edgar's foster mother died in February 1829 and he was granted leave to attend her funeral, but he arrived too late. In their mutual grief, Edgar and his foster father had a reconciliation, and his father agreed to pay a substitute so Edgar could be dismissed honorably from the army. He also arranged an appointment for him at West Point. Perry left Fort Monroe for what he thought was the last time.

But he returned to the fort in 1849, by which time he had become world famous, and he was paid to read his poetry and lecture on literature at the Hygeia Hotel adjoining the fort. One month later Edgar Allan Poe, the real name of Sergeant Major Edgar Perry died in Baltimore.

At the time of his death and for years afterward, it was believed that Poe had died of alcoholism and exposure, aggravated by years of near-starvation, resulting from bad habits begun when he was at the University of Virginia and Fort Monroe. Recently, doctors studying his case have come to believe that Edgar Allan Poe actually died of rabies.

Saving the Harvest
·1831·

Cyrus McCormick straightened for a moment to ease his aching back and wiped the sweat from his face. Cutting wheat was one of the hardest, hottest jobs done at Walnut Hill or anywhere else. It had to be done quickly, soon after the grain turned golden and matured, and before rain or wind came and beat it to the ground to rot.

Cutting was done in 1831 the same way it had been done for centuries all over the world. Humans bent, knife in hand, and cut the stalks. Then other humans gathered the cut stalks and took them out of the field to a hard surface, where the grain could be knocked free from the husks. Some harvesters used sickles—small curved knives—and could cut only half an acre of grain a day. Using a scythe—a knife almost as tall as a man, with a perpendicular handles—a worker could cut four times as much, two acres a day.

The McCormicks and many other farmers had added a row of bars called a "cradle" to their scythes to support the grain as it was being cut. This helped, but the extra bar made the scythes heavy. WIth this tool, a strong worker could cut three acres in a day. But the sun was hot, the work was exhausting, and the days were long. There must be a better way, Cyrus thought.

His father, Robert, had tried to solve the problem, inventing a harvesting machine that was pulled by horses. It could cut the grain if the land was perfectly flat and the grain was dry, but dampness or an uneven crop caused it to work poorly.

Robert had abandoned the "reaper" after fifteen years of effort and worked instead on other inventions and the running of the farm, the blacksmith shop, and the iron furnace.

Robert and his wife, Mary Ann Hall McCormick, both Scots, were practical, hardworking people who had prospered. Mary Ann was said to work as hard as any man, but she also surrounded herself with beautiful things. Both made sure their inventive son had as good an education as a boy in Rockbridge County, Virginia, could get in the early 1800s.

Young Cyrus had showed ingenuity in school and had worked alongside his father in the blacksmith shop. Now he set to work trying to determine why his father's reaper had failed and how he could make one that would succeed. He knew the machine's knife must move forward as well as perform a sawing motion, and he devised a reciprocating knife with a serrated edge. It clicked back and forth as the horse pulled the reaper forward. A divider bar separated the grain to be cut from that standing. To solve the problem of fallen or wet grain, Cyrus added a row of fingers that held the grain in position to be cut and a reel that lifted fallen grain. After the grain was cut, it would fall onto a platform, where it could be raked off by someone walking beside the reaper. The entire machine was set behind and to one side of the horse that pulled it. The horse walked on the stubble of the just-harvested row.

Working day and night with the help of a skilled slave, Joe Anderson, Cyrus pushed to get his reaper ready to test by the end of the harvest that summer. Cyrus had finished harvesting before the reaper was ready, but Robert left one small field for a test. Everyone on the farm came out to watch as the machine moved noisily across the patch of grain.

It worked, but Cyrus saw a few things he could improve. A few days later, he was ready to demonstrate the reaper again, this time in oats instead of wheat, on a neighbor's field. In one afternoon, the reaper cut six acres of oats, the work of six men with scythes or twenty-four with sickles. On that afternoon, Cyrus McCormick changed agriculture forever.

Again, Cyrus made minor changes in his invention, and the next year he demonstrated his reaper on a farm at nearby Lexington before a hundred spectators. Some hooted, but the reaper did its job superbly.

It took some time for the reaper to become widely used. Why didn't farmers who saw the reaper rush forward to buy what would save them hours of labor? For one thing, labor was cheap. Immigrants needing jobs poured into the North, and the southern states had slaves. For another, McCormick's invention came at the very beginning of the industrial era, when farmers were unused to machinery. Many still used wooden plows instead of iron and tended to think that what was good enough for their ancestors was good enough for them.

But Cyrus was determined to make and sell reapers. He wanted to save people from the backbreaking labor of cutting grain. He needed money to buy iron and to advertise, so his father gave him a tract of land to farm to raise the necessary money. It didn't work out so Cyrus tried raising money by operating an iron furnace. The work was so constant that he had no time to build reapers. Then came the Panic of 1837, when prices of both iron and farm produce fell. Farmers had no money for reapers. Cyrus lost everything except the one reaper he had made and the patent for it. Still he worked on.

Cyrus sold his first reaper for $50.00 in 1840, nine years after his first demonstration. That same year he sold two more, and the first purchaser furnished a glowing testimonial. Cyrus raised the price for a reaper to $100.00 and sold seven in 1842, twenty-nine in 1843, and fifty in 1844. Several people bought the right to sell reapers, and orders began to come in from outside Virginia.

Delivering a reaper in Virginia to another state was difficult. The reaper had to be taken by wagon to the James River for shipment to Norfolk, then by ship to New Orleans and by riverboat up the Mississippi, and again by wagon to the purchaser. Virginia was not the place for a reaper factory.

Virginia wasn't really the place for reapers, either. Its fields were too small and hilly for the reaper to be useful. When Cyrus made a trip out west, he saw where the future of reapers lay. In Ohio, Indiana, Iowa, and the Great Plains states his reaper could cut enough grain to feed the world.

Once Midwestern farmers saw the reaper, Cyrus began to get more orders. He had no trouble setting up agencies to sell the machines and licensing other factories to manufacture the reapers. But he had no control over the quality of production. He needed to build a central factory in the Midwest. Chicago, then only a muddy village, had railroads and was on Lake Michigan. Cyrus decided it was the right location.

Although Cyrus McCormick's design was not the first reaper patented, it was the first to have all the necessary features, and Cyrus became wealthy not only because of his invention but because of his business methods. He understood the importance of a written guarantee, of producing a well-made product, and of advertising. He also set a uniform price, eliminated negotiation, set up a system of sales agents, and accepted installment payments.

The five basic characteristics of Cyrus's reaper, with slight modifications, were used to make reapers for a century. Eventually tractors rather than horses pulled the reapers, but the method of cutting grain did not change.

Entertaining
the Queen
·1843·

In Ireland, the rollicking, music-loving Sweeney family was called McSweeney. When they immigrated, they dropped the "Mc" but not the love of music. One of the first immigrants from the family ran the popular Sweeney's tavern in Appomattox, Virginia, where folks could gather for fun and music.

Joel Sweeney's father was a wheelwright, a maker of wagons and barrels, and around the Sweeney home stretched fields of corn, wheat, and dark tobacco that flourished in the red clay soil of Appomattox and Buckingham Counties. A man could do well and support a family on such land or in a blacksmith shop making wagons and repairing farm tools. But Joel knew early on that neither kind of labor attracted him.

Whenever he could slip out at night or on Sundays, Joel Sweeney listened to the slaves on an adjoining plantation. When they didn't have to work, they entertained each other by singing, dancing, and telling stories that often included animal sounds like squawks, chirrups, and growls. Joel sat in the darkness, laughing at how lifelike their animal imitations were, watching their swaying bodies, and feeling moved by their melodic songs.

The slaves accompanied their singing with an instrument they called the "ban-jar." Joel would sit entranced, watching their dark hands holding the stem of the ban-jar and thrumming on its four strings. It didn't have a range of notes but was used mainly to keep the rhythm going.

Joel asked the slaves how they learned to make and play the instrument. From our ancestors, who learned to make it in Africa a long time ago, they said. It was a simple instrument, made by stretching four animal-hide strings across the shell of a dried gourd and attaching a handle. It wasn't difficult to play.

When he was thirteen, Joel made himself a ban-jar and learned to play it. Soon, however, he decided its sound was too monotonous. He wanted something that could play tunes as well as keep rhythm.

Joel noticed that many different sizes of gourds could be used to make a ban-jar. But some shells were too thick, others were too thin, and no two gourds made ban-jars that had the same sound. The Africans had used gourds because they were easy to grow and therefore free, but Joel realized he didn't have to settle for an irregular-shaped gourd. He was a wheel-wright's son. He could make a perfect instrument, as uniformly round as a wheel, with wood exactly as thick as he wanted it. And once he got it right, he could finish it with turpentine or paint.

Working patiently whenever farm work let up, Joel shaped and glued a lightweight wooden frame. Over this he stretched a circle of leather and secured it in place with tacks. The carved handle was smooth and graceful, with pegs for adjusting the tautness of the five strings. The African ban-jar had had only four strings. Joel called the fifth one a chanter. When he finished the instrument, he ran his fingers across the strings. The instrument sounded just the way he wanted it to, and it felt right in his hands.

The instrument was more melodic and versatile than the ban-jar. It seemed to be a new instrument altogether. He called it a banjo. The banjo is the only musical instrument to originate in America.

Joel also learned to play the violin, or the "fiddle." With his banjo and fiddle, he left behind the fields and wheelwright shop and became a traveling minstrel. He traveled about central Virginia, first attracting an audience among the crowds gathered for court days. He'd play "Listen to the Mockingbird" and whistle imitations of various Virginia birds. Joel cavorted in the dusty courthouse square or on the steps, playing and singing tunes he'd heard and inventing new songs. He never learned to read music and in fact said that a banjo didn't actually have notes. It was just played.

Joel was an instant hit. Stories spread that he was so talented with the banjo that he could play it with his toes and at the same time play the fiddle with his hands and blow into a harmonica. He was a one-man band.

Joel Sweeney earned the name "the Pied Piper of Appomattox" and "the father of American minstrelsy" (for introducing the blackface act as well as break dancing to American audiences). He was popular among blacks as well as whites and was the forerunner of the Christy Minstrels, Al Jolson, and vaudeville.

Earning his living full-time as a performer, Joel next joined a small circus and toured Virginia and North Carolina. He traveled with the circus for several years as its star. Then, as entertainers do, he wanted to test his act in big cities, to find out if he and his banjo would appeal to Northerners as well as Southerners. When the tall, dark-haired Virginian stepped out onto the stage and began playing in New York, Philadelphia, and other big cities, audiences applauded wildly. His act was as popular among the more sophisticated Northerners as it had been among his friends and neighbors in central Virginia.

In 1843, Joel, then thirty-three years old, headed for Great Britain. Again, he wondered if his music would appeal to Europeans or if they would look down on the folksongs, flamboyant dancing, and simple instruments. He joined Sand's Great American Circus. Their first appearance in Britain was at the Lyceum Royal Theater in London. Joel was billed as "Mister Sweeney, the celebrated Virginny Banjo Player." At the time, being addressed as "Mister" denoted respect; it was not a title given to every male as it is today.

From London the troupe crossed the Irish Sea to appear in Dublin, Cork, and Belfast, then journeyed north to Edinburgh and Glasgow. Then Joel was commanded by Queen Victoria to perform for her.

Joel played his banjo, sang the songs he'd created, and waited to see if the Queen would be pleased. She was. She laughed, clapped, and gestured for him to approach the throne. When he bowed before the petite, young queen, she asked him to become her court musician. Although he declined, Victoria gave him a money belt filled with gold coins in appreciation of his music and had a suit made for him.

Joel returned to the United States and continued traveling and playing music. He died of "dropsy" when he was fifty, on the eve of the Civil War, but others, including his brothers, played his music to bring cheer to the Confederate troops.

Here Lies Stonewall Jackson's Arm
· 1863 ·

In early 1861, Professor Thomas Jonathan Jackson was an unhappy, unpopular professor of artillery, optics, mechanics, and astronomy at Virginia Military Institute. Remarried after the death of his first wife, the deeply religious Jackson believed in predestination: Everything that happened to him was intended to happen. Conversely, one of his frequently stated maxims was, "You can be whatever you will." Guided by these two contradictory ideas, he became a fearless commander.

If the Civil War had not happened, Jackson likely would have passed the rest of his life as a teacher, spending his spare time boning up on unfamiliar subjects, practicing his lectures, and spending time with his daughter. Instead, he was thrust into leadership positions. The Civil War changed his life forever, and his death changed the course of the war.

At the First Battle of Bull Run, three months after the opening of the war, Confederate troops were fleeing until Jackson took the field and not only stopped the retreat but ordered an attack. When he raised his left hand, it was shot through. He tied it up with a handkerchief and kept fighting. Soon the Union forces retreated, overrunning the spectators in carriages who had come out from Washington to "watch the war." Supposedly, General Barnard Bee pointed out Jackson and cried, "There is Jackson standing like a stone wall. Rally behind the Virginians." Thus Jackson acquired his nickname.

After Bull Run, "Stonewall" Jackson was assigned to defend the Valley of Virginia, the "breadbasket of the Confederacy," a task he performed so brilliantly that military strategists still study his campaign with awe. A strict disciplinarian, he drove his men almost to the breaking point, but after each battle he said prayers of thanksgiving and always reminded them that God was with them.

In fact, Jackson's tactics were so effective that some military historians think that if the war had been fought only in Virginia, the Confederacy could have won. However, events elsewhere turned the tide. Jackson's part in the war lasted less than two years.

May 2, 1863, was a day of surprises, ironies, and tragedy. General Robert E. Lee divided his already outnumbered army, keeping part in Fredericksburg and sending the larger portion with Jackson to outflank Union General Joe Hooker's troops near Chancellor House.

Hooker caught sight of Jackson's troops and wrongly assumed that Lee was retreating. He sent part of his forces to attack the "retreating" forces, leaving a gap in his line. By this time Jackson's troops were in position, and two hours before sunset they attacked Hooker's army, charging out of the thickets into the midst of unsuspecting men preparing dinner or relaxing around a campfire, their weapons stacked to one side and the supply wagons close beside them. They were not ready for combat. Some scattered in panic, but others fought.

Fighting continued as darkness fell, although neither side could see the other. Most generals would have called off the fight and reorganized, but Jackson wanted to push ahead and force Hooker's army back to Fredericksburg. He rode out ahead of his army on his horse, Little Sorrel, and was accidentally shot by his own army, who could only make out shadows and thought he was the enemy.

Jackson took three shots, one in the right hand and two in the left arm, one of which shattered the bone above the elbow. He managed to hang onto Little Sorrel until two of his aides stopped the frightened horse and got the injured general off. As the fighting continued, with bullets flying and riderless horses shrieking frantically, it was important to get Jackson to safety and to a surgeon. He was put on a litter, but as the bearers were carrying him off one of them was struck and killed, and Jackson fell to the ground and was further injured.

Dr. Hunter McGuire, a Confederate surgeon, got Jackson onto an ambulance and gave him morphine for his pain. Jackson was uncomplaining but felt sure he would die. If he did, it was God's will, he thought. He accepted calmly the doctor's decision that the arm must be amputated and inquired about the course of the battle.

Jackson was taken to the field infirmary at Wilderness Tavern, where Dr. McGuire gave Jackson more morphine and later chloroform and amputated his left arm just below the shoulder. His arm was buried in a small family cemetery not far from the site of the Battle of Chancellorsville.

When Jackson regained consciousness, he complained of pain in his right side, where he'd been injured in falling off the litter. Dr. McGuire examined the area but could determine no wound. This was before x-rays, blood pressure tests, antibiotics, and other medical advances now taken for granted. Jackson's fall probably caused a rib to puncture his lung or caused internal bleeding. The amputation site and Jackson's bullet-shattered right hand both healed well, with no swelling or inflammation.

General Lee ordered that Jackson be moved away from the front to Guinea Station, and on Tuesday, May 5, he was well enough to be moved. His wife, Anna, was sent for and she came from Lexington, bringing their infant daughter, Julia.

Despite the healing of his wounds, Jackson grew weaker. Other doctors were sent for. When he saw them, he realized how serious his condition was. He comforted his wife and told her he was ready to die if it was God's will, requesting that he be buried in Lexington.

According to legend, Jackson's final words were, "Let us cross over the river and rest in the shade of the trees." Then he died peacefully.

When Jackson's body was taken through Richmond, accompanied by Confederate President Jefferson Davis and his cabinet, thousands turned out to mourn. General Lee called Jackson the world's best executive officer and said, "Jackson lost his left arm, but in him I lost my right."

In two years Jackson went from being a colonel teaching at a small military school to being a general known and revered throughout the Confederacy. He is the best-known Civil War commander, after Ulysses S. Grant and Robert E. Lee.

The Crater
· 1864 ·

By the summer of 1864, the Civil War, which both sides had optimistically thought would be over a few weeks after the first shots were fired at Fort Sumter, had dragged on for more than three years. Union General Ulysses S. Grant's plan to take the Mississippi River had succeeded, cutting the Confederacy in two. But despite a crushing defeat at Gettysburg and tremendous casualties at the Wilderness, Confederate General Robert E. Lee's Army of Northern Virginia still hung on.

Lee's army was dug in at Petersburg, Virginia, which had long been one of the most prosperous and important cities in the South, terminus of several roads and railroads and an important manufacturing center. Grant put the city under siege, gradually starving its inhabitants, but still Lee's army didn't surrender.

In late June, Colonel Henry Pleasants, a coal mine engineer and leader of a regiment of coal miners from Pennsylvania, devised a plan to break through the Confederate line, which was then only 150 yards from the Union lines. Because his men were skilled at tunneling and blasting, Pleasants proposed to tunnel under the Confederate fortifications. Black powder at the end of the tunnel could blow a hole in the Confederate defenses, and in the ensuing chaos Union forces could attack. The plan was approved and work started on June 25.

For over a month the miners dug the 400-foot-long tunnel. It was 4 feet wide at the bottom, 2 feet wide at the top, and 5 feet tall. Men working inside had to crouch, digging out earth and carrying it outside. At the tunnel's end they dug side galleries, forming a T-shape. The tunnel was finished on July 27, and four tons of black powder were carried inside.

Before dawn on July 30 Pleasants himself went into the tunnel, lit the 98-foot-long fuse and ran for the entrance, which was almost completely blocked with dirt to concentrate the blast.

The men waited for the explosion so they could rush in and kill Confederates, but nothing happened. Forty-five minutes passed. Finally two miners risked their lives to go in and check the fuse. Working in darkness because a lantern might have set off an explosion, they found the break, mended it, relit the fuse, and ran for their lives.

Just at dawn there was a rumble; the earth rose in a mound and then exploded like a volcano erupting. Black smoke and flames spouted from the hole and huge chunks of earth flew skyward, carrying along men, tents, cannons, everything. The resulting crater was 30 feet deep and 170 feet across.

More than 250 Confederate soldiers died in the blast and the position was devastated. The survivors ran in terror. The situation wasn't much better on the Union side. Some soldiers, terrified by the blast and the debris flying through the air, fled. Others who were supposed to pour in through the breach in the Southern line had neglected to level their own fortifications, so they had to clumsily climb out of deep trenches and up over an earthen wall.

Like curious sightseers at disasters everywhere, the Union army ran to the edge of the crater to have a look. Some began digging out half-buried Confederates, others scavenged among the dead and dying, and others just slid down into the crater to find out what was going on. The planned attack was a shambles.

Union Generals Ambrose Burnside and George Meade were far back in separate locations and unaware of any problems at the crater. They sent out runners, who had to make their way through the debris and confusion to determine what was going on and get back to the command post.

The attack had been expected to succeed within minutes of the blast, but it had not. The commanders ordered more troops to the crater site. They were to approach by a system of trenches the army had dug, which kept them down out of sight but also out of action and susceptible to an attack.

After the big blast, a few Confederates drifted back toward the crater, protected by a ravine, and began to organize themselves to fight. Confederate gun emplacements flanked the crater, and the guns pounded the Union lines. Union cannon fired back, tearing up the ground around the Confederates, but they were never able to silence the Confederate fire.

Meanwhile, Burnside and Meade sent each other angry telegrams, accusing each other of failure. At about this time, Meade decided to send in black troops. They had been trained for several weeks especially to lead the charge, but Meade feared bad publicity if they were sacrificed. Now that the attack was doomed, they were sent in.

The sun had risen and the day had become hot and humid. Union troops, packed into trenches and taking cover in the crater itself to avoid Confederate fire, began to pass out from the heat. The Confederate cannon dropped canister shot into the midst of the trapped men. Bodies and weapons fell on the packed masses in the crater and in the trenches nearby. The steep sides of the trenches and crater made it all but impossible to climb out, and the tunnel was blocked with dirt at the back end and filled with smoke and fumes.

The black troops had been told before the blast that their job was to run across the crater and take the high ground overlooking Petersburg. They tried. Taking heavy casualties as they ran along the ridge above the trenches, they regrouped and turned, shooting and clubbing the Rebels in the trenches. Then they leaped up onto the parapet and were shot. A few made it over and attacked in the ravine.

When the Confederates counterattacked, the black regiment broke and fled, just as their white compatriots had done earlier.

General Grant realized the battle was lost and ordered a recall. Meade sent word to Burnside, who still stubbornly thought he could win and thus did not sound the recall.

Men trapped in the crater sent runners for water, and the runners were shot or taken prisoner. Ammunition gave out, and the dead were searched for more. More than 200 men fainted from the heat.

The battle finally ended in early afternoon, eight dreadful hours after it had begun. The Union lost 3,798 men, many of them shot while trying to get back to their own lines. Pleasants was furious at how his well-planned scheme had gone awry. Burnside soon resigned.

The Battle of the Crater, planned to destroy the Confederates at Petersburg, was far more deadly to the Union.

No More Need to Roll Your Own
· 1882 ·

Tobacco has been a part of American life since even before the first colonists arrived in Virginia. The first tobacco was ground into snuff, wrapped into large, molasses-flavored twists for chewing, packed loosely into pipes, or rolled into cigars. Then several developments changed tobacco usage.

In the 1840s, smokers began rolling chopped tobacco in small bits of paper to be smoked. These "cigarettes" (little cigars) were easier to light than a pipe and more convenient. The entire thing could be smoked and thrown away. They were especially popular with soldiers and cowboys on the move.

Tobacco companies, seeing the possibility of wider markets, had their workers roll the tobacco into paper and seal it, but individuals in factories were not much faster at rolling cigarettes than smokers who rolled their own. Such a repetitive motion could surely be done by machine.

When James Bonsack, then a teenager, heard that Allen and Ginter Tobacco Company in Richmond was offering a prize of $75,000 to anyone who could invent a machine for rolling cigarettes, he decided he was the man for the job. His family operated a woolen mill near Roanoke, Virginia, and he was familiar with how machinery worked.

When Bonsack told his friends about his plan, they laughed, but he persuaded them to pool their resources to buy materials. When they'd made the machine, they could share the prize, he said. Bonsack himself made a workable rolling tube from sheet brass but did not at the time make the complete machine. His friends lost interest. He eventually bought them out and from then on depended on his grandfather to pay for materials, about $50.00 in all.

In 1878 Bonsack's parents sent him to Roanoke College at Salem to get an education and told him to put ideas of inventing a cigarette rolling machine out of his head. But he didn't. He wasn't interested in history and literature. He kept thinking about the cigarette machine and dropped out of college, to his father's disappointment. However, realizing that his son was serious about making the machine, Jacob Bonsack gave James a small workspace at the woolen mill. James's brother helped design the mechanism that fed material into the roller, and James himself devised the knife that cut the finished cigarettes.

James applied for a patent but discovered that Albert Hook of New York had patented a similar but less successful machine three years earlier. The Bonsacks decided to buy out Hook. Eventually the deal was closed, for $18,000. Jacob Bonsack thought this an outrageous price to protect something that had not yet proved itself, but he had faith in his son and put up the money.

James set to work completing the machine and loaded it onto a boxcar to ship to Allen and Ginter in Richmond. Disaster struck. The boxcar and the machine inside burned in the railyard at Lynchburg.

However, what looked like misfortune may have been a blessing. The insurance company paid Bonsack for his loss, and with the money he set to work building a better machine. He applied for a patent on it and had the parts and patterns cast in iron so he could produce many more rolling machines.

By now, James Bonsack and his family realized what a valuable invention they had. They formed a company to make and lease the machines. The Bonsack Machine Company, chartered March 27, 1882, issued shares of stock at $100.00 each, intending to raise at least $50,000. James was only twenty-three years old.

The first Bonsack cigarette-making machines were manufactured in France, but later the machines were made by Glamorgan Company in Lynchburg. According to Glamorgan's records, it cost $300.00 to manufacture each machine, and they were sold to the Bonsacks for $700.00–$800.00 each.

Allen and Ginter leased the first machine, and by 1884 the Bonsacks had seven machines in operation in the United States and seven in Europe. Each one was rolling as many cigarettes in a day as forty-eight people rolling them by hand could produce, and the products were all uniform. Everybody was profiting, and the Bonsacks' company began paying dividends to its investors.

An entrepreneur who saw the vast potential of the Bonsack machine was James Buchanan Duke, who with his brother had formed Duke Tobacco Company, later American Tobacco Company. Duke first leased five of the machines in 1882. His costs for making cigarettes dropped from 80 cents per thousand to 30 cents, thanks to the Bonsacks' machines.

The machines didn't always work as they should, and Duke wanted to keep his going, so he hired away Bonsacks' main mechanic. He next secured a contract giving his company exclusive use of Bonsacks' machines. Not content with this, the American Tobacco Company in 1895 went to court against the Bonsacks' company, claiming it had a monopoly in restraint of trade. As a result, the Bonsacks lost the exclusive rights to make parts of their own machines. Duke then bought the machines it had been leasing.

The Bonsacks were part of a group that formed United Cigarette Machine Company in England. They owned 75 percent of the company's stock. The company was liquidated in 1916, after having paid half a million dollars in dividends to its investors. By this time Bonsack & Company had the rights only to the machine's automatic feeding device, which is still used in making cigarettes.

For a time Glamorgan was making money manufacturing the cigarette machines, tobacco farmers were making money as there was more demand for cigarette tobacco, the government made money because every packet of cigarettes had to have a government revenue stamp, and the Bonsacks made money leasing their machines. But the part of this operation that made the most money was James B. Duke and his American Tobacco Company. He became immensely wealthy manufacturing cigarettes using a machine invented by a Virginia boy.

Seeking the
Beale Treasure
· 1885 ·

One day in 1885 a thin pamphlet, "The Beale Papers," appeared in the shop windows of bookstores in Lynchburg, Virginia, describing a treasure allegedly buried in nearby Bedford County. The author was James Ward, who stated in his introduction that the Beale papers had been given to him by someone else who had gotten them from Robert Morriss, a Lynchburg hotel keeper. Thomas J. Beale had given the papers to Morriss, who described the circumstances surrounding them.

According to Morriss, Beale arrived at his hotel in January 1820, accompanied by several friends who traveled on to Richmond. Beale remained at the hotel until the end of March, when the friends returned to Lynchburg and he left with them.

Morriss described Beale as tall, strong, and "swarthy," popular with both men and women, to whom he was unfailingly polite.

Beale returned to Lynchburg two years later, in January 1822, and left again at the end of March. When he left the second time he gave Morriss a small, locked iron box, asking him to keep it until he called for it. Morriss put the box aside and thought little of it until a letter arrived from St. Louis dated May 9, 1822.

The letter, from Beale, stated that he would be away about two years and that the box contained extremely valuable and irreplaceable papers. If Beale had not returned by 1832, Morriss was then to open the box by cutting off the lock. The papers inside would be unintelligible, Beale's letter said, because they were written in code. However, a key had been prepared and addressed to Morriss, to be mailed in June 1832.

Morriss never received the key. He waited not just ten years but more than twenty, hoping that Beale would return. Finally, he opened the box in 1845. Inside were three sets of papers, each covered with strings of numbers, and another letter, written January 4, 1822. In it, Beale explained that he'd chosen Morriss because of his integrity and good reputation. The papers would tell the exact location of a great treasure, describe what it was, and give the names of the group who had found the treasure and whose heirs would share it. Morriss was to dig it up, divide it into thirty-one shares, keep one for himself, and distribute the other thirty to the group of heirs.

Morriss tried working out the code using various historical documents and even chapters of the Bible, settling eventually on the Declaration of Independence as the key. Using that, he decoded enough of the letter to determine that the treasure was iron pots filled with gold, silver, and jewels mined at a location north of Santa Fe. According to the letter, Beale had taken the pots at night and buried them secretly 6 feet deep, at a location 4 miles from Buford's Station in Bedford County.

Morriss was unable to work out the other codes, and after years of trying he turned them over to someone else, who turned them over to Ward.

Soon after Ward's pamphlet was published, the printing plant burned. The original letters and papers from Beale were never made public. With a title like "The Beale Papers," the little pamphlet didn't sell well, so no more copies were printed. Little attention was paid to the possibility of a treasure for a dozen years.

Then in 1897, Clayton and George Hart began a search for the treasure after Clayton's boss, Newton Hazlewood, asked him to type up a list of numbers that he said led to a treasure.

Hazlewood, an employee of the Norfolk & Western Railway, was later quoted as saying he'd tried to persuade Ward not to publish the pamphlet. Why?

Is there a Beale treasure? Did he bury his treasure only to have someone discover it and take it away secretly? Did Beale even exist, or was he a fictional character created by Ward?

There was a Thomas Beale of the right age, born in western Virginia, the illegitimate son of Chloe Delancy and Thomas Beale, Sr. That Thomas Beale operated a tavern in New Orleans, married there, and had a family. When Thomas Jr. went to New Orleans to locate his father, his father was dying and his stepmother wanted nothing to do with this Virginia son. If Beale did find a treasure, he would not have wanted it to fall into the hands of his stepmother and her children and might well have trusted an older, childless man like Robert Morriss.

Morriss was well known and believed to be honest. The hotel he ran in Lynchburg later became the Arlington Hotel. Beale might well have stayed there. Ward also lived in Lynchburg. His grandfather is said to have fought a duel with a Thomas Beale.

If the treasure existed or exists, how did Beale bring it all the way from Santa Fe to Bedford County without attracting the attention of thieves? Assuming he brought it to Virginia, how was it buried? Did he have help? The area around Buford's Station was then heavily wooded, making it difficult for wagons to travel. Beale would have needed a string of pack mules to carry a treasure as heavy as the one he described.

Or was it all an elaborate hoax, and if so, whose? Did Morriss write the letters and make up the code? Did Ward? In the pamphlet Ward claimed not to be the author, but then, what author would claim a hoax? Perhaps Hazlewood wrote the pamphlet, or the two worked together. Ward and Hazlewood lived near each other in Lynchburg; they were both Episcopalians, both Masons, and both familiar with Buford's Station.

According to the paper supposedly decoded by Morriss, relying on the Declaration of Independence, each number stood for the first letter of a word at that order in the document. For example, the first word is "when," so 1 would mean "w." However, the word "when" shows up more than once, so other numbers could also mean "w." Having decided on a message, the author may have then painstakingly located the correct letters in the Declaration of Independence to supply the "solution." The other two papers full of numbers may well be gibberish, a string of completely random numbers relating to no document.

For more than a century treasure hunters have been coming to Bedford County, to a place now called Montvale, seeking a treasure trove of gold, silver, and jewels estimated to be now worth more than $21 million. They come from nearby cities and counties, from other states, and even from foreign countries, drawn by the possibility of instant riches. They seek out old maps and rent local backhoes to dig and helicopters to fly them over the site. The Beale Treasure has been featured on network television programs and in a variety of magazines. Every time it receives publicity, another flurry of treasure seekers comes to Bedford County.

An association has formed of people who think they can break the code. They share information with each other and are using computers to decipher the message. Will they succeed? A 4-mile radius from Buford's Station covers thousands of acres. That's a lot of digging for something that may not exist. But if it does exist, there is a lot of wealth at stake.

The Carroll County Shootout
· 1912 ·

Hillsville, Virginia, today is a pleasant, busy small town, equipped with the usual fast food and motel franchises at the junction of U.S. Highways 221, 58, and 52. It is one of the gateways to the Blue Ridge Parkway and the Appalachian Trail. In 1912 those highways were narrow roads, the Parkway had not yet been built, and hiking was not a sport but the necessary way to reach a destination.

The sleepy town, county seat of Carroll County, Virginia, was in 1912 the site of one of the most sensational trials in the state and a shootout that has been called the Carroll County Massacre.

In 1911 the newly elected county officials were Republicans, whereas the numerous Allen family members were Democrats. After the Allens protested that they couldn't count on Republicans for justice, Judge Thornton Massie made Floyd Allen and H. C. Allen members of a special police force.

Trouble between the Allens and Carroll County law enforcement began in September 1911, ironically at a church service. Two brothers, Sidna and Wesley Edwards, attended a service conducted by their uncle, Garland Allen, their mother's brother. During the service, someone beckoned Sidna to step outside. When he didn't return, Wesley stepped outside to see what was wrong and found his brother involved in a fistfight.

Wesley took on several of the opponents, evening the odds against his brother.

The brothers were arrested, charged with disturbing the peace, and released to await trial. Deciding to await it elsewhere, they went to North Carolina and got jobs. The sheriff found out where they were and sent two deputies to bring the Edwards brothers back to Carroll County for trial. The deputies reportedly returned them with their hands tied.

As they passed through Fancy Gap, Virginia, another uncle, Floyd Allen, saw them and demanded that the deputies release his nephews into his custody. They weren't guilty of much, just a little fight of the kind all young men sometimes get into, he said. They weren't dangerous. And after all, he was a member of the Special Police Force. He attempted to release his nephews.

The deputies pulled their guns and ordered Allen to stand back. He grabbed one deputy's gun and smashed it against a rock, knocking the deputy against the rock as well. While that deputy was unconscious, the other ran, and Allen cut his nephews free.

The next day Allen took the boys to the sheriff's office and arranged bond for them, guaranteeing they would stay put this time. Not surprisingly, Floyd Allen himself was arrested for complicity in the escape of prisoners. He too was released on bond.

In spite of late winter weather and poor roads, family members and spectators packed the Carroll County courtroom when Floyd Allen's trial began on March 13, 1912. Many in the courtroom were armed, including the court clerk, the prosecuting attorney, the sheriff's deputies, Allen's family and friends, and even Floyd Allen himself. Evidence was heard and the court adjourned for the day.

The next morning the foreman of the jury announced that they had found Floyd Allen guilty as charged. His attorney objected and moved that the verdict be set aside. Judge Massie indicated he would hear the motion the following day. In the meantime, Allen was to be held in jail.

Allen stood and declared that he wasn't going to jail. A shot rang out, followed by a hail of bullets from several directions. People screamed and ran or screamed and dropped to the floor. The deadly fusillade was over in a few seconds. The defendant, Floyd Allen, was injured, along with the clerk, one of the jurors, and several spectators. Dead were Judge Massie, the prosecuting attorney, one of the jurors, and a spectator. The courtroom was blood-spattered and littered with bits of wood and spent shell casings.

Allen was taken across the street to a small hotel where his wounds were tended, then taken to jail. He was now charged with first-degree murder. Other members of the Allen family, all accused of planning the shooting and participating in it, fled and hid. Virginia's governor offered a reward of $3,000.00 for the capture of the Allens. Newspapers called them "desperadoes" and reported the captures as they happened.

Floyd's son, Claude Swanson Allen, surrendered two weeks later. Sidna Allen, Floyd's brother, and Wesley Edwards, one of the nephews whose fistfight had started the whole mess, hid out for several weeks and then went to Iowa to work, where they were found and arrested. They were brought back to Virginia six months after the courtroom shooting.

Meanwhile, Floyd Allen was back in the courtroom in May 1912, a scant two months since his first trial. This time he was accused of first-degree murder in the shooting of the prosecuting attorney. Allen denied it. He pointed out that he had been shot first, and there were over a dozen bullet holes in the rail where he had been standing. He admitted to shooting back, in self-defense.

The jury found him guilty. The penalty was death.

In July, Floyd's son Claude was tried for murdering Judge Massie. He pled not guilty, claiming that his family liked the judge and had considered him a fair man. Like his father,

Claude Allen admitted drawing his gun. He shot at the clerk after seeing the clerk shoot his father, he said.

Claude Allen's first trial ended with a hung jury. A second trial later the same month resulted in a guilty verdict and a sentence of death. Father and son were to be electrocuted November 22, 1912, but the date was postponed. Other family members also faced trial and received long prison sentences. Floyd's brother Sidna Allen was sentenced to thirty-five years, Wesley Edwards to twenty-seven years, and Sidna Edwards to eighteen years in prison.

Throughout the state thousands of people signed petitions asking that Claude's life be spared. He had only been defending his father, supporters said, as a son should.

The governor ignored the petitions and on March 28, 1913, both father and son were put to death. More than 12,000 people viewed their bodies at the Richmond funeral home where they were taken, some bringing flowers. About 5,000 attended the double funeral in Carroll County.

Only a year and two weeks elapsed between the courtroom shootout and the deaths of the accused. Justice was swift, but some would say it was blind in this case.

Mr. Peanut
· 1916 ·

Peanuts were brought to Virginia from West Africa and have been grown in Virginia since colonial times, but it took an Italian immigrant, Amadeo Obici, to turn the lowly legume into a million-dollar business.

As a child, Obici immigrated alone from near Venice to the United States to live with his uncle in Pennsylvania. For several years he worked with his uncle; then, as a teenager, he went to Wilkes-Barre and operated a fruit and peanut stand. He was a clever salesman. By the time he was twenty-one, Obici had earned enough to bring his widowed mother, his sisters, and a brother to the United States.

Obici noticed that people bought more peanuts than fruit from his stand. Moreover, fruit was perishable, whereas peanuts kept well for months. Shrewdly, he bought a peanut roaster and a snack stand of his own. Then, instead of waiting for customers to come to him, he mounted the roaster and peanuts on a wagon and drove about the countryside selling fresh-roasted peanuts. He was called the "Peanut Man."

One good idea led to others. Peanuts were durable and portable, so why not package them in small quantities that could be shipped to other towns and cities? Obici tried it, and sales went up. He recognized Americans' love of convenience. To make peanuts easier to eat, why not shell them at the factory, then roast the nuts and package them? This innovation was another success. Obici had come up with a "fast food."

Obici experimented with salting the peanuts to make them tastier. The salt stuck better if the skins were removed, so Obici began boiling the peanuts, skinning them, and then roasting them in hot salted oil. Next, he noticed that Americans ate a lot of sweets. To appeal to these candy lovers, he created chocolate-covered peanuts; they also were a hit. Everything Obici did increased sales.

By 1906 Obici was so successful that he could no longer manage all the business alone. He formed what would become the Planters Peanut Company along with his future brother-in-law. The business was incorporated in Pennsylvania as the Planters Nut and Chocolate Company.

The next big change was a move to Virginia. Since the company used Virginia peanuts, and advertised them as such, it made sense to move closer to the source. In 1913, Obici bought a small factory in Suffolk, Virginia, the middle of the peanut-growing region. As he had with his other endeavors, he soon began expanding the company. There were still offices in Pennsylvania, and Obici opened up offices in other cities as well, but Suffolk became the headquarters.

Always looking for ways to make more people aware of his product, Obici decided in 1916 to hold a contest for a trade-mark design. He wanted something that would be easily rec-ognizable and would appeal to children and adults alike. Obici offered a $5.00 prize, and students began drawing. The win-ning entry, a sketch of an in-shell peanut with arms and legs, a smiling face, and a cane, was created by fourteen-year-old Anthony Gentile of Suffolk, who called his creation "Mr. Peanut."

Obici liked the design and had a commercial artist add to the original. Mr. Peanut was given a Lincoln-style top hat, a monocle in one eye, white gloves, and black-and-white spats on his feet. These additions made him look more classy, Obici thought. Mr. Peanut began to appear in magazine ads and on the cellophane bags of salted peanuts, which Obici advertised as the "5 cent lunch." Soon Mr. Peanut was one of the best-known symbols in the world.

People loved Mr. Peanut. His image showed up everywhere. The perky goober decorated Christmas cards and cocktail napkins. For the desk, there were Mr. Peanut pen and pencil sets and letter openers. Mr. Peanut appeared in the dining room as the stem of colored glassware and in child-sized knife, fork, and spoon sets. Condiments came to the table in Mr. Peanut salt and pepper shakers. Bakers could make cookies with a Mr. Peanut–shaped cutter. There was a large, stuffed Mr. Peanut doll, and any children who had coins to save could drop them into the hat of a green, plastic Mr. Peanut bank. Smokers could view Mr. Peanut in the bottom of their ashtrays or on a cigarette lighter embossed with Mr. Peanut's image. And for serving peanuts at home, there was an elegant silver nut server with Mr. Peanut on the handle.

One of the most obvious displays of Mr. Peanut was the Peanutmobile used during the 1920s. It was a two-seated car shaped like a huge in-shell peanut. Emblazoned on its side were the words "Planters Salted Peanuts" and astride its trunk was a replica of Mr. Peanut, larger than the driver. Peanutmobiles were used by company sales representatives making calls on stores and distributors. Sales reps also carried business cards in the shape of a peanut. School groups touring the Planters factory were led by someone dressed in a papier mâche Mr. Peanut costume with a 2-foot-tall top hat.

Mr. Peanut, the symbol, and the real Mr. Peanut, Amadeo Obici, enriched Suffolk, making it the "Peanut Capital of the World" and bringing millions in wealth to Virginia farmers.

In 1937, when the Great Depression had dampened many businesses, Obici optimistically launched a new advertising campaign. In New York's Times Square he built a 10-foot-tall figure of Mr. Peanut, outlined in lights that blinked off and on so that Mr. Peanut appeared to bow. Other lights spelled out the company's well-known name.

Besides the familiar salted peanuts, Planters also made peanut brittle, peanut butter, peanut oil, and the Jumbo Block, a tabletop-sized candy bar made by hand from peanuts and chocolate. All bore the familiar Mr. Peanut logo.

Obici began an annual celebration called the National Peanut Exposition. At the 1941 Exposition the "Peanut Queen," whose full title was Miss Arachie Hypogea (the Latin name for peanuts), wore a long dress covered with in-shell peanuts hand-stitched onto the dress. It weighed 75 pounds. Also featured at the festival were shapely young women wearing two-piece bathing suits covered with peanuts. Obici knew how to generate publicity for his products!

When the original 1913 Suffolk plant was replaced by a new one in 1994, Mr. Peanut went along. Fourteen cast-iron replicas of Mr. Peanut line the fence outside the main building. Peanuts are still grown in Suffolk, and peanut products are still processed there. In the "Peanut Capital of the World," Mr. Peanut reigns as king.

An Island of Ponies
·1925·

The Chincoteague ponies, auctioned annually at Chincoteague, Virginia, and made famous by Marguerite Henry's book *Misty of Chincoteague,* are neither ponies nor from Chincoteague. They actually live on Assateague Island and are horses, diminutive because of centuries of inbreeding.

Horses are not indigenous to North America and certainly not to barrier islands. Stories are told about horses swimming to Assateague Island from a Spanish shipwreck, perhaps a Spanish pirate ship, in the 1500s. It's a romantic tale, but there is another, more likely explanation for the horses' presence on the island.

Soon after Jamestown was settled, colonists claimed land on Virginia's Eastern Shore and built homes and plantations on the flat, fertile land. There were no roads then, but rivers and bays were the highways of the colony.

Sometimes animals would be penned on the Common, the land shared by all settlers. This proved unsatisfactory because some settlers pastured too many animals, so the common pasturage was discontinued. Each family had its own livestock, but sometimes still let them roam freely, and free-roaming animals became a nuisance. Laws permitted trespassing livestock to be shot, so the settlers turned to the barrier islands for pasture. Islands made a perfect corral, because animals could only escape by swimming away.

As other parts of Virginia were settled, some of the Eastern Shore residents moved away, heading westward along with other pioneers, leaving their livestock on the islands. Others gave up farming and turned to fishing. Gradually they acquired title to the islands, and eventually they began to herd the wild animals ashore and sell them. No new animals were added to the stock on Assateague Island to add vigor to the herd. Inbreeding and the privations of life on the island have led to the small size of what are now called ponies.

Assateague Island is about 12 miles long, with a small, sandy beach facing the Atlantic Ocean. Otherwise, it is fringed by marshes that attract migratory birds. In midwinter the island barely has enough grass to keep the ponies alive. Fresh water comes only from rainfall, and mosquitoes and other insects are always a problem.

The small horses on Assateague Island were first described in an article in the *Farmers' Register* in 1835, and even then the "horse-pennings," as they were called, had been held for some time. People would go to the island in scows; leap out; chase the frightened horses into pens; load up those to be sold; and then enjoy dancing, singing, and eating—in what the author writing in the *Register* called a "half-savage festivity."

At the end of the nineteenth century, Chincoteague became the center of the oyster industry in Virginia, and its population grew tenfold. Then the railroad was extended down the Eastern Shore, and tourists flocked to Chincoteague for sport fishing and summer vacations. All remaining ponies were herded onto Assateague.

Then the automobile came, and Chincoteague was linked to the mainland by roads and bridges. There was little need anymore for horses, especially not for small stunted "ponies" to pull carts.

But children love ponies, and from time to time there would be a roundup of the colts. People would come from afar in cars and trucks, buy ponies, and take them away. The market was no longer dependent on local buyers.

The pony swim became an annual civic event in 1925. Two disastrous fires—one in 1920 that burned a tourist hotel and a dozen houses and a second that burned businesses and homes on the western side of the island in 1924—convinced Chincoteague's residents that they needed a fire department, and men volunteered for the duty. But they needed equipment. How could they raise the money for it? How about a carnival? And how about selling ponies at the same time, someone suggested. They weren't doing anybody any good, just multiplying out there on the islands. Nobody even owned them. They were just there, like birds and other animals on the islands.

After going through some red tape, the fire department acquired ownership of a herd of Assateague ponies and began planning for their fund-raising carnival.

In 1925, the first modern "pony penning" took place. Volunteers, now called "saltwater cowboys," swam their own horses across the strip of water from Chincoteague to Assateague, rounded up all the ponies, and made them swim to Chincoteague. Here they were herded along the main street, watched by admirers, and corralled into a prepared pen. The next day, the auction began. It was part of a two-week carnival, complete with rides, sideshows, and food sales, and it benefited not only the fire department but all the residents who owned hotels or boarding houses or who had anything to sell to tourists.

The event was so successful that it was held again the next year, and the next, and the tradition continues to this day. Every year in the last week of July, these small horses are herded together and made to swim across the narrow channel, their way directed by a fleet of boats. Children come with their parents and watch with all the anticipation of Christmas Eve as the ponies run past. "I want that one!" "The brown one's mine!" they exclaim as they spot a sleek-sided pony with a long mane.

The ponies are separated out into those that will be sold

and the stallions and mares that will be taken back to Assateague for breeding. Because of the limited pasturage, only 150 ponies are kept, and because of wildlife management laws, no outside stock can be introduced to the island. As a result, the ponies are becoming more inbred, all sharing the same DNA. They are all susceptible to the same diseases. But for now, they are well cared for.

At the sale the bidding begins. Sometimes prices go as high as $5,000.00, and disappointed children sigh when their parents drop out of the bidding. But they will have another chance next year.

Ham for a Play
·1932·

A Virginia actor, Robert Porterfield, was on tour with a play, *Cyrano de Bergerac,* but he was one of the lucky ones. All over New York, aspiring actors and actresses, dancers and musicians auditioned or walked the streets, only to see signs on theaters that read "Closed." It was 1932 and the Great Depression was gripping the nation. Times were hard.

Times were equally hard for farmers, Porterfield noticed as he traveled from state to state across the United States. Farmers were destroying crops, pouring out surplus milk, and reducing herds because it cost more to produce food than they received when it was sold. Porterfield decided there must be some way to get that food to people who needed it but had no money to buy it. Or maybe he could bring the hungry actors to the food producers.

Porterfield had an idea: In earlier eras of hard times, people bartered their produce or skills for goods they needed, with no money changing hands. Farmers in his native Washington County, Virginia, had never seen professional theater, only amateur productions performed by their children at school or church and an occasional traveling vaudeville act. Maybe they'd be willing to barter their produce for admission to a play, he thought. Thus was born the Barter Theater.

When Porterfield's tour ended, he too was out of a job. It was time to put his plan into action. He persuaded twenty-two out-of-work actors and actresses to join him in Abingdon, the county seat of Washington County. There was an old unused theater building in Abingdon, and across the street was a grand mansion that had been turned into a girls' school. The actors could stay there or at Porterfield's nearby family home, Twin Oaks.

With some doubts, but with no better prospects, the twenty-two actors and actresses arrived. Porterfield himself arrived in the baggage car of a train, guarding the flats of the play *Rose Marie* that he'd persuaded the road company to give him.

Using lumber and old nails from a derelict local barn, Porterfield's stage crew got busy assembling the scenery for their first play, *After Tomorrow*. Others practiced their lines and put up advertisements for the play: "With vegetables you cannot sell, you can buy a good laugh." For those who had money, the admission price was 35 cents.

On June 10, 1933, the play opened. To Porterfield's delight, a large audience arrived, bringing jams and jellies, eggs, ham, freshly baked cakes, potatoes, beans, and even a pig. The Barter Theater presented six more plays that first summer. Porterfield reasoned that the more frequently he changed plays, the more frequently audiences would attend, bringing along their produce. Locals told of one man who led his cow to the theater, milked 35 cents worth of milk, and left the cow outside for his wife to "milk her own ticket."

Comedians joked that the only way to determine if the Barter Theater was a success was to weigh the cast at the beginning of the season and again at the end. By this measure, Porterfield's plan was a success: The Barter company collectively gained 305 pounds. There was in addition $4.35 in cash and two barrels of jelly in the storeroom.

If barter could work with audiences, why not with authors? Porterfield told the playwrights he had no money for royalties but would pay them a Virginia ham for the right to present each play. When George Bernard Shaw objected that he was a vegetarian, Porterfield sent him a case of Virginia-grown spinach instead.

Reporters wrote about the Barter Theater, critics arrived to view plays, tourists came, and the Barter's reputation spread. When summer ended, the troupe went on the road, presenting plays all over Virginia, wherever there were suitable stages to perform on, always accepting food in return for tickets. The Barter became known as the State Theater of Virginia.

As economic times improved in Virginia, more people paid cash for admission and fewer paid in produce. Porterfield wanted to put the company on a sound financial footing, and in 1940 he appealed to the Virginia legislature for financial support, pointing out that the Barter Theater was important in attracting tourists to the state. It offered some nightlife.

"What kind of nightlife do you mean, young man?" one suspicious senator asked.

"The kind you can go home and talk about," Porterfield answered.

"Give him the money!" the senator declared.

In return for financial support, the Barter was to produce twelve plays in Abingdon each summer. For the remainder of the year the company would tour in Virginia. In 1948 the Barter company was invited to Denmark to present *Hamlet* at Kronberg Castle.

Besides entertaining generations of Virginians and attracting tourists from other states and countries, the Barter Theater has been the proving ground for many of America's best-known actors and actresses. By 1960 Porterfield had produced more plays than any other living producer. That meant a wide range of opportunity for thespians to hone their skills. Actor Gregory Peck, for example, played three parts in one play, *Lee of Virginia:* John Brown in the first act, Stonewall Jackson in the second act, and Ulysses Grant in the third act. Other famous Barter alumni are Patricia Neal, Hume Cronyn, Lisbeth Scott, Ernest Borgnine, Ned Beatty, Gary Collins, Barry Corbin (Maurice in *Northern Exposure*), Larry Linville (Frank in

M*A*S*H), John Spencer (Leo in *The West Wing*) and Jim Varney ("Ernest").

To attract leading stars to his corner of Virginia, Porterfield established the Barter Theater of Virginia Award for the most outstanding performance by a U.S. actor or actress during a given season. The "trophy" was a ham, a platter to eat it from, and an acre of land near Abingdon. The award has been won by Ethel Barrymore, Louis Calhern, Henry Fonda, Tallulah Bankhead, and Mary Martin.

Robert Porterfield died in 1971, but his Barter Theater, which forged a link between poor farmers and poor actors, brought thousands of visitors to Abingdon and western Virginia, and launched many careers, is still going strong, presenting well-staged drama.

Richmond's
Famous Dancer
· 1938 ·

On June 30, 1938, a parade wound its way through Richmond. At the conclusion the mayor unveiled the portrait of a smiling black man, probably the most famous black person in the United States at that time. "I declare this to be Bill Robinson Day, and this theater is named in his honor," the mayor said. Richmond was proud of its native son.

Most people knew Bill Robinson as Bojangles, who had danced his way across the movie screens of America and won the hearts of American moviegoers. During the Depression, when most people had trouble making ends meet and one-quarter of American men were unemployed, Robinson was earning $5,000.00 a week. He was generous to friends, to other entertainers, and to his native city. One of his very practical contributions to Richmond was four traffic lights for the intersection of Adams and Leigh Streets. On an earlier trip he had noticed that it was dangerous for school children to cross there. He was sympathetic, because he had once been a child in Richmond.

Robinson's life was the stuff of legends. Poor and orphaned, he left Richmond for Washington, D.C., in the late 1880s, at the age of nine. He worked first as a stable boy but soon got a child's part in a traveling minstrel show. The star, Eddie Leonard, a white dancer who was also from Richmond, befriended Robinson and taught him some of his dances. In

1894 Robinson teamed up with comedian George Cooper, and the two formed a vaudeville act that toured until the economic slump of 1907 put them out of work.

Robinson returned to Richmond, where he worked as a waiter at the Jefferson Hotel. It was a comedown for the entertainer, but it was one of the few jobs then open to black men. One day he accidentally spilled soup on a customer and apologized. The customer grudgingly accepted the apology. The next day Robinson was dancing on the sidewalk outside the hotel when the customer came out. He was Marty Forkins, a New York theatrical agent. He watched the dancing, entranced, then gave Robinson his card and some money and told him to come to New York. Forkins was Robinson's agent for the next forty years.

Throughout the following two decades, Robinson toured the United States, dancing in theaters and nightclubs, pulling in crowds wherever he danced. In 1928 he was added to the cast of a show called *Blackbirds in Harlem* and became at age fifty an "overnight success." He went on to appear in *Brown Buddies* in 1930, *Blackbirds of 1933,* and *Blackbirds of 1934.*

Even more success lay ahead for Robinson. In the 1930s he appeared in four films with Shirley Temple, the box-office champion child star, and in ten other films. He appeared on radio shows as well and had his own dance studio. Although he had never taken dancing lessons, Robinson taught some of Hollywood's leading dancers, including Shirley Temple. The two worked well together, each adding to the other's appeal: the smiling white child and the smiling black man. In most of these films, Bojangles played a subservient role, and some blacks complained that he was letting down his race by accepting such roles, but he kept dancing, kept smiling, and kept earning big fees.

Although he accepted second billing in films, in real life Robinson protested segregation and once used a pistol to convince an unenlightened coffee shop attendant to serve him and some friends. Later, when Robinson heard that black troops were being segregated in Harlem camps in World War II, he went to the mayor's office and called President Roosevelt from there. The camp segregation ended.

In addition to dancing, Robinson also ran backwards as fast as some people could run forwards. He was timed at 13.5 seconds for running backwards one hundred yards. On his sixtieth birthday in 1938 he ran backwards for sixty blocks up Broadway.

Robinson kept in shape by dancing every day, practicing relentlessly while wearing specially made wooden-sole tap shoes. He was so fond of vanilla ice cream that he ate it at every meal, even breakfast, but the exercise kept him slim. He didn't smoke or drink, and his face was so smooth and unlined that at sixty-five he believably played a romantic lead opposite Lena Horne, then in her twenties, in *Stormy Weather.*

Robinson welcomed visitors from Richmond and was always willing to help younger entertainers, remembering that Eddie Leonard from Richmond had helped him when he was young and needy. When asked how things were, he always answered, "Copasetic, just copasetic," meaning "Everything's fine."

He was generous not only with his money but with his time as well, appearing at thousands of benefit performances for charity. Always loyal to Richmond, he even appeared in a show for the inmates at Henrico prison, just outside the city.

Aside from a hot temper, Robinson had only one fault: gambling. He once said, "These feet earned four million dollars, and these hands threw away two." By the time of his death from a heart attack in 1949, he had spent, given away, or gambled away his entire fortune. Once the wealthiest black man in the United States, he died broke. There wasn't even enough in his bank account to pay his funeral expenses, but theatrical friends raised the money, and his funeral was grand.

In 1970 Robinson hometown honored him again. The site where his four stoplights had hung was turned into a park, named Bill Robinson Square. A 9-foot-tall statue of Robinson doing the stair-step dance he made famous in films keeps his memory alive in Richmond.

War Comes
to Virginia
· 1942 ·

Whaen word of the Japanese attack on Pearl Harbor
reached the mainland United States, coastal cities feared that
they too would be bombed. Surely Norfolk would be a target,
Virginians thought. After all, it was (and is) home to America's
largest naval base, and nearby are a Coast Guard base, Fort
Story, Camp Pendleton, and the Norfolk Naval Shipyard in
Portsmouth.

Within a week, on December 13, Norfolk had its first
scheduled blackout to conserve energy and hide the city from
any potential air strikes, but Portsmouth stayed alight. On December 29, civilian defense coordinators ordered a seven-city,
sixteen-county blackout, which was very effective. Christmas
lights, which were just becoming popular for decorating trees
and houses, were turned off. Windows were shrouded with
blackout curtains, and shopkeepers turned off their store light-
ing.

But as time passed and no bombing occurred, Virginians
relaxed. True, men were being drafted into military service,
many products were rationed, and news of battles came from
Europe and the Pacific. But in Virginia the coming of war actually brought prosperity. Crops were in demand, all that farmers could produce. Camps and barracks had to be built in a
hurry, providing jobs. Norfolk's population swelled, and every
available housing unit was occupied.

Summer came, and in spite of war, those who could went to the beach. The weather was hot in June 1942, but there was almost always a cooling breeze coming off the ocean. Lying on the sand, basking in the sun, or swimming in the surf, it was easy to forget danger. There were a few oily spots on the sand, remnants of oil slicks that at times had covered the beach during the spring. Out on the horizon on June 15, a convoy of merchant ships appeared, steaming northward toward the port of Norfolk. That was not unusual either, for Norfolk was one of the most important East Coast commercial ports as well as the point of embarkation for naval ships headed for Europe.

The beaches weren't as crowded on June 15 as they had been the previous day. It was a Monday, and the weekend visitors had gone. Late in the afternoon of the 15th, sunbathers were gathering up their books and blankets, folding umbrellas, and herding children out of the water. Suddenly, a few minutes after 5:00 P.M., there was an explosion, then another. Everyone on the beach turned to look out at the water. Doors and windows flew open in houses and hotels up and down the beach.

Out on the ocean, calm just a few minutes before, water spurted up and fell, and a wave rolled toward the shore. Smoke poured from a crippled tanker less than 6 miles away. It had gone down by its stern in 54 feet of water until it touched bottom and its bow thrust upward.

Torpedo! The word was passed from person to person. It must be a torpedo. The explosion was louder than the depth charges to which beach residents had grown accustomed. That meant German submarines, called U-boats, were nearby.

Despite the danger, the Coast Guard had to get to the stricken vessel. They launched a 24-foot-long motor surfboat and headed out into the ocean.

Just then a second explosion erupted at the stern of another tanker. Undeterred, spectators streamed to the oceanfront, standing along a 3-mile stretch for a view of the action.

Coast Guardsmen, soldiers, and sailors attempted to hold back the crowd.

Within half an hour, the first survivors of the crippled ships were rescued and taken to the Naval Operating Base. Eventually, the oil-covered body of the single fatality, a ship's engineer, was brought ashore and taken to the Coast Guard station at the beach.

The hundreds of sightseers continued to watch as America fought back. A blimp arrived and hovered over the scene, searching for survivors that had been missed. Planes from the Naval Air Station flew low, searching for the marauding U-boats and dropping depth charges that shook buildings onshore. Some onlookers reported seeing a sub come to the surface and then disappear after one of the depth charges, presumably blown to bits. However, eight depth charges produced nine explosions, which was an indication that the ships had encountered mines set by U-boats, not a U-boat itself. Other planes came, as well as various surface naval vessels that maneuvered among the lifeboats and the remains of the convoy.

As darkness fell, the crowd slowly dispersed, returning to their homes or hotels. The sunken tanker remained, its bow pointing skyward. Already, attempts were being made to tow the second, less damaged tanker to port for repairs.

The only mention of the ship sinkings in the following day's newspaper was a seven-line article with the headline: "Crowds at Virginia Beach Hear Sound of Explosions at Sea; Navy Withholds Information." But anything witnessed by hundreds of people could not be kept a secret, and on June 17 there was a full account of the incident, including interviews with the survivors.

In contrast to the single fatality on the two ships, four Norfolk area residents drowned over that weekend and another was electrocuted while wet from swimming.

Among the crew of the first tanker attacked were three merchant seamen who were experiencing their second rescue at sea. The trio had earlier been on another tanker that was attacked and sunk. The steward on the second ship was upset because the attack had overturned pots and pans in the galley, dousing him and ruining the dinner. He'd planned a special menu that included meatloaf, pork chops, and veal.

The crews of the two ships were for the most part lucky. Not so fortunate was a trawler, *Kingston Ceylonite,* which was leading two other ships northward along the coast later that same night. It took a direct hit and sank in two minutes. Twenty of its crew of thirty-six died. Bodies and body parts washed ashore for several days. They were buried in southern Virginia and northern North Carolina.

There was no beachfront relaxation anymore. War had truly come to Virginia.

A Plague Strikes
Southwest Virginia
· 1950 ·

The summer of 1950 began like other summers in Wytheville, a town of 5,500 in the valley of southwestern Virginia, between the Blue Ridge and the Allegheny Mountains. School was out, the public swimming pools were open, and plans were well underway for summer camp and vacation trips. Children played softball and ate ice cream cones from the drugstore; teenagers hung out together as teenagers did everywhere. People worked at their jobs and attended church. In the evening adults sat on front porches and discussed the situation in Korea, but that was so far away. They talked about the upcoming annual horse show and dedication of a new "Lakes-to-Florida" highway, Route 21, that would pass through Wythe County.

No one could have predicted that this summer would not be like others. A dreaded disease would strike down more than a hundred victims, most of them children. The town of Wytheville was the epicenter of an outbreak of polio that was the worst in the nation that year. According to the National Foundation for Infantile Paralysis (the original term for polio) Wytheville had fifty times more cases of polio than it should have had statistically for a town of its size.

Polio was no stranger to the United States; former President Roosevelt himself had been stricken. The disease was feared above all other diseases. It struck mostly children, killing randomly, leaving the survivors paralyzed or crippled. A mother could see that her children ate right and brushed their teeth, and a father could work to provide a comfortable home and a good example to his children, but there was no protection against polio. Wytheville itself had had an outbreak six years before, with twenty-four cases. Most of the survivors still lived in Wytheville, some of them limping slightly. When polio struck again in 1950, they recognized the symptoms.

The first cases appeared in early July. Children complained of headaches, felt feverish, and sometimes had difficulty breathing. Perhaps it was polio, perhaps not. Only a spinal tap test could determine for sure. Local doctors did what they could, then transferred the suspected cases by ambulance to Memorial and Crippled Children's Hospital in Roanoke, an 85-mile ride. Parents were told that if they suspected polio, they were to put the child in bed and contact a doctor.

By July 12, Wytheville had sixteen suspected cases of polio, ranging from a two-month-old baby to a twenty-four-year-old man. Despite this adult case, health authorities still considered it a problem of children. But they took precautions for adults as well. The municipal pool was closed, telegrams were sent to the governor and other dignitaries postponing the dedication of the highway, and the horse show was rescheduled for a month later. Anyone younger than sixteen was forbidden to attend the movies or to loiter on the streets. Parents were urged to cancel trips and summer camp, but some panicked parents considered fleeing town before their children were struck down.

A pall hung over the town. Playgrounds were empty; children were kept at home and made to play quietly in their own backyards. Even church gatherings were canceled, and Sunday school lessons were broadcast over the radio. But these measures were no protection, for no one knew then how polio spread. Was it through drinking water, food, touching someone who was infected? There was no cure and no vaccine. Some died when paralyzed muscles stopped their breathing. About all the hospital could do was put the most-affected victims on respirators to keep them breathing.

On July 12, doctors in adjoining Carroll and Grayson Counties issued their own alert, warning against travel to Wytheville as well as letting children become overtired. Parents were to keep children away from anyone they did not usually associate with and to postpone having dental work done. These precautions were drawn up by the National Conference of Recommended Practices for the Control of Poliomyelitis.

The following day, July 13, officials in Wytheville announced that the epidemic seemed to be subsiding. There had been two deaths, twelve positive cases, and three suspected ones. No new positives had been reported in Wytheville, but a case in Southampton County brought Virginia's statewide total to fifty cases.

This announcement, alas, was premature. By August 5, polio had spread beyond Wytheville into the surrounding area. Wythe County recorded 118 cases, fifty-eight of them in the town, and thirteen deaths. Victims poured into the Roanoke hospital from Giles, Buchanan, Pulaski, Washington, and Tazewell Counties, and of the eighteen respirators sent out to all of the United States by the National Foundation, thirteen went to Roanoke. Meanwhile, the state's total cases rose to 261. The epidemic was not limited to young people; one southwest Virginia victim was fifty years old.

As August began, more events were canceled. The Boy Scouts decided not to hold their annual camp at Claytor Lake. A joint Baptist-Methodist Bible School was called off. Families decided to forego reunions for 1950. In addition to reporting on the epidemic in the newspaper, the staff of the *Southwest Virginia Enterprise* posted a list of victims on a bulletin board outside.

The civic leaders of Wythe County set up a treatment center in the Veterans Memorial Home in Wytheville for survivors who would need special care after their return from the hospital. Most of Wytheville's polio victims had bulbar polio, which affected their breathing. If patients survived a week with no impairment to their respiratory system, chances were good for a full recovery.

By this time, some of the first victims were being returned home to be cared for by their families. Physical therapists were sent by the March of Dimes Foundation to instruct parents in caring for their children, and five health nurses were added to the two in Wythe County. Caregivers had to give bed baths, turn the patients, and apply hot packs to the twisted, weakened limbs to ease the pain. Beds were equipped with special footboards to pull the legs out straight.

The disease had struck in clusters, often several members of a family. Two of three Archer children and two of their cousins were stricken, four of six Taylor children sickened and one died, four Joneses got the disease. In one family, an eleven year old who had survived polio in 1944 helped nurse her stricken brothers and sisters. Her mother had also had polio in her own childhood. Was it hereditary?

When the summer of 1950 ended, so did the polio epidemic. No one knew what began it or what ended it.

The United States suffered a major polio epidemic in 1952. Jonas Salk's polio vaccine, tested between 1952 and 1954, was not ready for widespread use until 1955.

Bigger than
the Brink's
·1955·

Shortly before closing time on Friday, December 16, 1955, more than twenty bank examiners walked unannounced into Commonwealth Savings and Loan Association in Norfolk, Virginia. They had been alerted by an anonymous letter from a friend of a bank employee that something strange, perhaps theft, was going on. An agent stood behind each employee until the day's work was checked. Only then could the employee leave. The last to have her day's work checked and leave was Miss Minnie Mangum, assistant secretary-treasurer, the second in command at the bank and the person who actually ran the establishment.

On Monday, Mangum's maid called the bank to say Miss Mangum would not be in. Nor did she come to work on Tuesday. That in itself should have alerted bank officials, if they had not already discovered the theft, because Mangum had never taken a vacation in twenty-seven years and often came to work on weekends. On Tuesday the police drove to her home in Portsmouth to ask for an explanation for large sums of missing money.

Mangum had worked for Commonwealth since 1927, and during that time she stole nearly $3 million—more than was taken in the infamous Brink's robbery.

After the auditors had made a complete survey of Commonwealth's records, police arrested Mangum outside her lawyer's office on December 29. Even the booking officers fingerprinting the plump, sixty-one-year-old woman could scarcely believe she could have masterminded such a huge theft. She wiped the fingerprinting ink off her well-manicured fingers, and when reporters questioned her, she said calmly, "I have no statement to make at this time."

When the news of her arrest on December 29 broke, people who knew Miss Minnie were astounded. She was a quiet, gentle person, they said, a Sunday school teacher, a good neighbor who was generous to the needy. How and why had such an unassuming person managed such a vast crime?

The how was easily explained. The why never was.

Because of family difficulties, Minnie Mangum dropped out of school in the seventh grade, took a correspondence course in bookkeeping, and took a job as a clerk at Commonwealth. She had little social life. Despite her lack of formal education, she had a keen mind for math and management and soon made herself indispensable to Commonwealth. The bank president was a super salesman but not especially interested in the day-to-day management of the business. And Miss Minnie was very dependable, very loyal, never taking time off for herself. She was so good at her job that she was profiled in the business sections of local newspapers in the early 1950s.

At first, she stole small amounts. She'd write checks to friends and rubber stamp them with the bank president's signature. As she grew bolder, the amounts became larger. In her last year at Commonwealth, she embezzled $600,000. Auditors found cash stuffed in various drawers and files in her office and estimated that of the amounts she'd stolen, at least half a million had been cash. She'd walked out with it in her pocket and fudged the books to cover the loss.

Miss Minnie made certain she hired only young, inexperienced staff, fresh out of high school. If any of her employees got too nosy, she'd fire them.

How did Mangum escape auditing so long? She developed a cadre of janitors who worked at various Norfolk financial institutions. They'd tip her off—for a fee—when auditors were in the area. This gave her time to remove the deposit cards of customers whose balances totaled the amount currently missing. Her math was so good and she was so alert to what she was doing that the two amounts always matched. After auditors examined the books and found that they balanced, Miss Minnie replaced the cards.

Why didn't someone notice her spending? The 1950s were a time of prosperity, especially in Portsmouth, and as a single woman earning $6,000.00 a year, she could afford a few luxuries or generous gifts. The main reason, though, was that no one saw the big picture. Who would turn her in? Certainly not the recipients of a new car or a loan at an especially opportune time.

What did Mangum do with the money? No Swiss bank accounts for her, nor did she spend it on herself. She had a reputation for being a penny pincher, never tipping when she ate out. She wore the same dowdy clothing year after year. Instead of pampering herself with things, she bought for others.

Mangum was called a modern-day Robin Hood, stealing from big business to give to the poor. She did give generously to her church, contributing thousands, but basically she used the money to buy friendship. She financed businesses and new homes for thirty-two friends and forty-three relatives and bought for them a total of eighty-five cars. She also gave lavish parties for friends' weddings, baby showers, and other occasions, and she ordered thousands of dollars worth of photographs of these parties. She often arrived at a friend's house laden with gifts, for no special occasion. Needless to say, her circle of friends grew.

After her arrest, Mangum deeded over her house and all her belongings to Commonwealth, and lawyers went after her friends and family who had received stolen money, but little of it was ever recovered. More than a million dollars was never accounted for.

The jury found Mangum guilty of making a false bank report, and she pled guilty to embezzling $2.8 million. She was sentenced to twenty years in the Goochland State Prison for Women. She served nine years before she was paroled; parole had been denied three times. During her time at Goochland she earned a high school diploma and managed the prison library. Who better to keep records? Mangum lived only two years after her release and would not talk about the embezzlement.

Two results of her embezzlement were the bankruptcy and subsequent takeover of Commonwealth Savings and Loan and a reform of the banking laws to make sure that no one else could ever carry out such a massive embezzlement.

When word of her crime reached the national media, calls came in from around the country and around the world. Everybody wanted to know why. A psychiatrist testifying at her trial said that she had a "severe character neurosis that impels her to carry out antisocial acts that are against her best interests."

Miss Minnie Mangum never explained why she stole the money.

Camille's Destruction
· 1969 ·

Nelson County, Virginia, residents paid little or no attention to the news of a dangerous hurricane, named Camille, approaching the coast of Mississippi in mid-August 1969. Those who followed weather news felt sorry for coastal residents and were grateful that they themselves were safe deep in the mountains of Virginia, hundreds of miles away from danger.

Like most hurricanes, Camille began as a cloud cluster off the coast of Africa early in August. By the time it struck the U.S. mainland, it was packing winds of nearly 200 miles per hour, and its central pressure was the lowest ever recorded by airplane. Clearly, it was dangerous. A mass evacuation took most coastal residents out of harm's way, but some died, and hundreds of homes were destroyed when Camille struck.

The winds abated as the rain-heavy storm moved up the Mississippi River and was downgraded to a tropical depression. Weather forecasters predicted that the depression would wear itself out over the mountains and would become just another rainstorm.

Then Camille turned eastward, crossing over the Blue Ridge Mountains of Virginia on the night of August 19, 1969, changing the lives and the terrain of Nelson and Rockbridge Counties forever.

The Blue Ridge Parkway roughly parallels the boundary dividing these two mountainous counties. Apple orchards dot the hillsides and the shallow, clear streams bubble along through fields and forests. Rockbridge is cut by the Maury and

South Rivers; Nelson has the Tye, Piney, and Rockfish Rivers and numerous creeks. The James River winds through Rockbridge and forms the southeastern boundary of Nelson. Both counties are thinly populated by hardy people who have lived in the area for generations. As in most mountainous areas, flat land is scarce and precious and lies mostly along the creeks and rivers, where most people built their houses and their towns. This was their undoing.

It was hot and humid that August afternoon. It had been a rainy month, and the ground was already soggy, so no additional rain could be absorbed. People unsuspectingly went about their usual summer routines—working in stores and factories, picking peaches, canning tomatoes, cutting grass that had grown tall from so much rain, tending cattle—unaware of the tragedy in store for them.

Just as darkness fell, Camille crossed into Virginia, and as it reached the Blue Ridge it began dumping its massive load of water, drenching Rockbridge County, then Nelson, beginning soon after 9:00 P.M. Twenty-eight inches of rain fell in the next eight hours, most of it in five hours, a record that the Weather Service calls a "catastrophic phenomenon." The hapless residents of Nelson County had no warning of what was to come, could not have comprehended the immensity of it, and would not have been able to escape the destruction and death even if they had been warned. Many tried.

Rain fell not in drops, but in sheets so heavy all the oxygen was sucked out of the air and birds drowned sitting in trees. The worst of the storm came at midnight, when people were in bed trying to sleep. Flooding knocked out the telephone lines and then electric power, so warning each other was impossible.

The little rivulets that trickle down the mountains to form creeks became raging torrents. The shallow creeks filled and spread to many times their usual width and depth.

Death and destruction were random. People attempting to escape by car were swept away; others who slept unsuspecting in their homes were also swept away. In Massies Mill, the Presbyterian church was demolished, but the Episcopal church still stands, although its church organ was found in another county when the water receded. The Raines family car stalled and they tried walking to a road they knew led to higher ground. But first they had to cross Route 56, wading in waist-deep water in the dark. The fourteen-year-old son, Warren, was following the family. He saw them by a flash of lightning and walked toward them. When the lightning flashed again, they were gone. Of a family of nine, only two sons survived. Later, they saw that a neighbor's house had lodged against a tree and diverted the heaviest water around the Raines house. If they'd stayed home, they would have been safe.

The Huffman family on Davis Creek was the hardest hit, losing twenty of its members in three generations. Thirty of their neighbors and friends were also killed. Most of the victims there and elsewhere in Nelson County weren't drowned but were crushed or buried by debris.

On Route 29, the main highway north and south through Nelson County, a bridge washed away, but traffic came on anyway. One driver whose car plunged into the swollen river managed to free himself and climb back onto the highway. He tried to flag down oncoming traffic, but no one stopped. He watched helplessly as other cars dropped into the water and were swept downstream.

Even those who sought high ground weren't safe. Soil on the mountains is only a few inches thick, and it was already water-logged. When the flood came, the earth slid, pushing boulders, splintering trees, and reshaping the hills. Survivors who smelled the raw, wet earth knew what it meant: No place in their county, not even the high ground, was safe on that dreadful night.

When daylight finally came and the rain ended, the dazed survivors looked out on a desolate world that outsiders knew nothing about yet. The sheriff had managed to get a message to the adjoining county in the midst of the downpour, only to be told that he needn't worry, the James River would not crest at the Nelson border for another day! Now he sent out messages telling the grisly news. As the outside world awoke to the horror, helicopters flew over and camera crews detailed the destruction. Word came that help would be slow; the highways were washed away. Somehow, the Mennonites from Augusta County, whose own area had also been hit, managed to get into Nelson to begin the grim task of finding and identifying bodies. The work went on for weeks after the water receded. Crews walked shoulder to shoulder, searching for a scrap of clothing, a hand, or a body-shaped mound that signaled a victim buried in silt and debris.

The flood swept on down the James River, swamping Richmond and eventually the Tidewater, carrying bodies and wreckage out into the Atlantic.

The final death toll is uncertain. In Rockbridge County the town of Glasgow was destroyed and twenty-three people died. Nelson recorded 125 dead, including twenty-three who died on Route 29. Eight of these were outsiders and were never identified. Thirty-three victims have never been found and are still listed as missing.

The land has mostly healed. Trees have grown, covering the scarred hillsides. Every autumn apples and the beauty of colored leaves draw visitors to this rural county. A ski resort in Nelson has upscale houses, but the few industries that were there in 1969 have closed and their buildings stand derelict. Once-flourishing towns are no more. Memorials and tombstones mark the lives of those killed by Camille.

Virginia's Master Spy
· 1985 ·

John Walker started the white van and headed onto Interstate 64 from Virginia Beach. On the seat beside him were a plastic garbage bag that held a few items of trash and a sealed bag of classified documents from the USS *Nimitz*. He was heading for a rendezvous with an agent of the Soviet KGB, as he had done so many times before.

At Richmond he turned north on Interstate 95, not realizing he was being followed by a series of cars driven by FBI agents and that a plane overhead was tracking him.

For months the tip-off about a spy had been ignored, but FBI agents Robert Hunter and Joseph Wolfinger took it seriously. The tip-off had come from Barbara Walker, John's angry ex-wife, an admitted alcoholic with reason to want revenge on her ex-husband. Still, she seemed to know in detail how the spying setup worked. The agents decided to follow up on the tip, even though FBI officials in Washington had dismissed her letter as worthless.

Hunter and Wolfinger put a tap on Walker's phones and staked out his house and boat. After weeks of frustration, the listening paid off. They heard him telling a girlfriend that he couldn't attend his aunt's funeral on May 18, a Saturday, and later telling associates that he would be in late on Monday. They had his schedule; he would make the drop on Saturday or Sunday.

They shadowed him all day Saturday as he played tennis, watched television, and washed his van. Then, on Sunday, he drove north, and they followed him to Maryland. Walker made two drops on a rural road, a soda can as a signal and the garbage bag full of secret Navy documents. The FBI unwittingly picked up both and almost ruined the bust. Still, they had the evidence, with his fingerprints all over it. They arrested him, ending a spying career that had covered nearly twenty years and had given the Soviets America's most crucial military information.

Within hours after Walker's arrest, the FBI arrested his brother Arthur, his son Michael, and his friend Jerry Whitworth. Walker had corrupted his friend, his brother, and son and had even tried to persuade his daughters to join the military and spy. He saw other persons only as tools. When he was questioned, he complained that they were all weak people who had let him down.

John Walker had dropped out of school as a teenager and joined the Navy because his brother had, but John found something at which he excelled. He earned five promotions in five years. He pulled submarine duty and was assigned to work with secret and cryptographic materials.

John stole his first documents in December 1967. He was living in Norfolk, in debt from buying a house and a money-losing bar in South Carolina, which he'd left Barbara to run. He was a watch officer in the message headquarters for the Atlantic Fleet. Almost all messages were encrypted, and the code was changed daily. Walker copied the key list for the coming month, drove to the Soviet embassy in Washington, and walked inside, expecting at every moment to be arrested. He made a deal with the Soviets to deliver information, codes, and wiring diagrams for encryption machines on a regular basis in return for $500.00 to $1,000.00 per month. He also sold information on ships' positions and plans for warfare, in short, everything the Soviets wanted. He put the lives of all U.S. naval personnel in jeopardy for his greed.

John brought his family to Norfolk, rented a lavish apartment, and spent money recklessly. He told Barbara he had a second job, then planted a syringe in a desk to make her think he was dealing drugs for money. Later she found a map and drop instructions and confronted him. He admitted being a spy and took her along on a drop. If he were ever arrested, she'd be implicated too and couldn't testify against him.

In his second year of spying, John was transferred to San Diego, where he met Jerry Whitworth.

In 1971 John was put in charge of all cryptographic materials on the USS *Niagara Falls,* and the KGB raised his pay to $4,000.00 per month. In 1973 John forged his own security check and got away with it, but he knew there would be another check every five years. He needed to get out of the Navy and find someone else to carry on. That person was Jerry, who had been assigned to the satellite communications center on Diego Garcia Island. John told Jerry he was spying for Israel and taught Jerry to photograph documents.

John was assigned to Norfolk, and Barbara finally divorced him after years of adultery and abuse. She and the children moved to Maine, and when John stopped paying alimony and child support, they lived in poverty. John, meanwhile, was living high on spying money: a boat, a plane, a fancy apartment, travel, a bevy of young women. He met his Soviet handlers in exotic places, and once took his mother along to smuggle the money back. His brother Arthur, who worked for a defense contractor, came onboard, and his son Michael joined the Navy and became a radioman, a perfect setup for spying.

Meanwhile, Jerry Whitworth, John's most valuable recruit, decided to quit spying. John previously had always managed before to talk him out of quitting.

Barbara had threatened for years to report John, but he always persuaded her not to, claiming that she wouldn't be believed anyway. Then she asked John for $10,000 in back alimony so she could attend college. John refused to give her the money, and she contacted the FBI, not knowing her son was also spying. She told the FBI that Michael had tried to talk her out of reporting John, so they began surveillance of Michael as well and caught him.

Arthur Walker and Jerry Whitworth received life in prison. Michael Walker, who had only been paid $1,000.00 for the documents he stole, paid with the loss of his career and twenty-five years in prison. John Walker received two life terms.

Ironically, the man who masterminded the most serious espionage in U.S. history and who had sold out his country and his family for more than a million dollars had not expected to receive any prison time. He fully expected that the CIA would approach him and ask him to be a double agent, giving misinformation to the Soviets.

Virginia Elects
a Governor
· 1989 ·

Doug Wilder had been running for office for twenty years, in a state where the pundits told him he didn't have a chance. Virginia had been the capital of the Confederacy, the last government address of Jefferson Davis, and L. Douglas Wilder was an African American, the grandson of slaves. But now he felt that the highest office in the state was within his grasp.

From the state Capitol, he could look out on the city of Richmond, where he had been born and which had been his home for all but half a dozen years of his life.

Wilder said that his family lived in "gentle poverty," but it was not poverty as most blacks, and many whites as well, experienced it during the Depression. The Wilders owned their own home, which had indoor plumbing at a time when many of both races still had outdoor privies. His father was employed when one-quarter of America's workers were not. His parents emphasized the importance of education in getting ahead. Complaining or protesting was not the way; education was.

Douglas early demonstrated the persuasiveness that would take him so far in politics. He sold copies of the *Richmond Planet,* a black newspaper, door to door, selling so many that he won a train trip to New York.

When Douglas and his siblings were growing up, everything was segregated: schools, hospitals, movie theaters, libraries, water fountains, transportation, and even store elevators. In 1948 the first black man was elected to the nine-member city council, in a city where 42 percent of the inhabitants were black, more than any other city in the South.

Douglas enrolled at Virginia Union University, planning to become a dentist. Tuition was only $100.00 per semester, half that for students who maintained a C average. Wilder maintained a C average, in spite of partying, participating in sports, and joining a fraternity. He also worked as a waiter at the Westwood Club and at the Jefferson Hotel, serving whites-only groups.

When Douglas Wilder graduated from Union in 1951, the "police action" in Korea was in full swing, and he was unable to avoid being drafted. In Korea one of his buddies was killed, and another, a white soldier, pushed Wilder to safety and was himself killed. Wilder was part of a two-man team that took twenty prisoners, for which he was awarded the Bronze Star.

Back home in Richmond, Wilder worked first as a letter carrier and then as a toxicologist at the state medical examiner's office. But he wanted to use the G.I. Bill. He liked debating, had an almost photographic memory, and was a good speaker. It would be law for him.

Although the University of Virginia admitted blacks to its law school, the state paid the tuition of any black law students who chose to go out of state. Wilder chose to attend Howard University in Washington, D.C.

Wilder didn't get involved in civil rights demonstrations as a student or later as a lawyer. His job, he thought, was to get demonstrators out of trouble afterward. As a trial lawyer Wilder prospered and began to gain publicity. This brought him in contact with whites whose support he would need when he went into politics.

That time came in 1969. He considered it a "now or never" situation and decided to run for Virginia senate. Wilder got the support of a group of wealthy young Democrats and announced that he would run. A white candidate, former Lieutenant Governor Fred Pollard, also announced he too would run. If the Democrats chose Pollard, Wilder said he'd run as an Independent, splitting the Democratic vote and giving the election to the Republicans. The Democrats decided not to decide: Both Wilder and Pollard were "certified as good Democrats." Wilder won. He received nearly all the black votes and a sprinkling of white votes as well.

How would the Virginia senate receive the first elected black senator? To Wilder's pleased surprise, he was accepted courteously by all, even warmly by several well-known segregationists he had dreaded working with. Perhaps they hoped he would fade into anonymity, but if they did, they were disappointed. The well-dressed, dapper Wilder drove a Mercedes convertible and soon attracted attention by objecting to Virginia's state song, "Carry Me Back to Old Virginny." Even though it had been written by James Bland, a black man, the song contained phrases that twentieth-century blacks found demeaning. (Eventually a contest was held to choose a new song, but none has been chosen yet.) He also repeatedly introduced bills to make Martin Luther King Jr. Day a state holiday.

Wilder learned what all successful politicians must learn, the art of compromise, a "you vote for my bill and I'll vote for yours" attitude. When blacks objected that Wilder was not voting "black enough," he responded, "Just because black is beautiful doesn't mean white is ugly."

During Wilder's first twelve years in the senate, Virginia had Republican governors, the first Republicans ever elected in the state. Then in 1981, Democrat Charles Robb won the gubernatorial election. Before the election, he had considered Wilder a rival, but Wilder kept out, not running himself or endorsing any candidate until after Robb secured the nomination.

Wilder, whose appearance had become more flamboyant (Afro hairdo, gold necklaces, and mod clothing) began to tone down in preparation for the 1985 election. He announced that he would run for lieutenant governor and started building up support. Mary Sue Terry, a white woman, announced for attorney general, and Gerald Baliles, a white man, announced for governor. Despite opposition, the three were nominated and called themselves the "Rainbow Coalition." Each appealed to a different portion of the electorate: blacks, white women, and white men.

Wilder left behind his Mercedes, borrowed a station wagon from a car dealer, and campaigned across the state, shaking hands with hundreds of thousands of people, playing the part of the poorly financed underdog. The entire team won, and news media from around the world descended on Richmond to interview Wilder, who now held the highest political office that any black in the United States had achieved.

The lieutenant governor is primarily responsible for presiding over the senate and casting tie-breaking votes. Wilder took advantage of his celebrity in office to raise money and prepare for the next election.

In 1989 L. Douglas Wilder was elected governor of Virginia. Even now, more than a decade later, he is still the only black ever elected governor of a state, and his triumph is especially noteworthy in Virginia, capital of the Confederacy.

Looking Forward
and Looking Back
· 2000 ·

As the year 2000 began, Virginians took special notice of their history. In April archeologists announced that they had found evidence of settlement in Virginia that went back not just to 1607 but to a culture that flourished near Richmond 17,000 years ago. This would predate the Clovis, New Mexico, settlement and cast doubt on the theory that America was populated by wanderers who crossed a land bridge from Asia.

The evidence was discovered by accident at a site called Cactus Hill, when a load of sand being dumped on a logging road was found to be filled with ancient artifacts.

This finding, after seven years of digs, made headlines for one day and then went unnoticed as Virginia prepared for OpSail 2000, a glorious gathering of sailing ships from around the world.

•••

It's natural that the Hampton Roads harbor (originally named "The Earl of Southampton's Roadstead") would be one of the sites chosen for OpSail 2000. Hampton Roads is one of the world's best natural harbors, leading ships from the Atlantic into the mouth of Chesapeake Bay and the James and Elizabeth Rivers. Ships have always played a mighty role in Virginia history, from the three that brought the first settlers to Jamestown, to the French fleet that assured American victory against the British in 1781, to the Battle of Craney Island in the War of 1812, to the Battle of the Ironclads in the Civil War. Hampton Roads is home to the Norfolk Naval Base, the Navy Amphibious Base at Little Creek, the Coast Guard Base at Craney Island, the Norfolk Naval Shipyard in Portsmouth, and several private shipbuilders.

OpSail 2000 wasn't intended to impress anybody with America's naval strength. It was a grand party, international and multiracial. Ships and tourists came from around the world.

All of the Virginia coast was involved. Ships would be berthed for the long weekend in Hampton, Portsmouth, Norfolk, and Chesapeake after their triumphant entry into the harbor on June 16. Churches and schools adopted individual ships and extended hospitality to the crews. The Soviet Union had been dissolved during a previous parade of sail, and the Soviet sailing ship was left stranded in Hampton Roads, its crew unpaid and hungry. Residents and businesses had donated food and drink and enough fuel to see the ship home. This time, hospitality would be arranged beforehand. St. John's Episcopal Church in Portsmouth adopted the *Faire Jeanne,* a tall ship from Canada, and arranged a barbecue for the crew. The ship was delayed elsewhere and never arrived. The church, with dozens of pecan pies and bushels of food ordered, managed to adopt two smaller ships, and the party went on.

June 16 dawned and the seagoing wayfarers gathered off the coast, ready for the U.S. Coast Guard cutter *Eagle* to lead them in. More than forty sailing ships from seventeen countries hoisted sails in the morning haze and glided majestically past an estimated two million spectators on the 30-mile route to Norfolk's waterfront.

The largest ship was *Kruzenshtern,* from Russia, at 376 feet. Almost as large was the Chilean 371-foot *Esmeralda,* which had an unlucky past. Her sister ship, *Juan Sebastian de Elcano,* from Spain, was only a foot shorter. Most popular was

Dewaruci from Indonesia, whose crew sang and danced to the delight of spectators along the route. *Gazela,* the oldest and largest wooden square-rigger still sailing, was launched in 1883 as a Portuguese cargo ship. She is now part of the Philadelphia Maritime Museum and is a "movie star," having appeared in several films and television documentaries.

Ships also came from Poland, Ukraine, Ecuador, Brazil, Canada, the Netherlands, Germany, Portugal, Uruguay, Italy, and Venezuela. One of Italy's participating ships was the beautiful *Amerigo Vespucci,* named for the cartographer for whom two continents are named. This steel-hulled ship is a replica of the wooden-hulled warships that once plied the world's oceans.

The constellation of ships began to move, accompanied by a flotilla of smaller vessels, nearly everything in Hampton Roads that would float. Everyone wanted a close-up look, and seats on boats went for big prices. The haze lifted, and the wind died. The sails had to be furled. By the time the sailing ships reached Craney Island, they were moving by motor power. Instead of glorious sails taut in the breeze, spectators saw masts.

• • •

Another ship had a more successful move. On December 7, 2000, the World War II battleship USS *Wisconsin* was moved from refurbishing grounds at the Norfolk Naval Shipyard to her permanent berth beside the Nauticus museum on the downtown Norfolk waterfront.

Wisconsin, the last of the big battleships made during World War II, was commissioned in late 1943 and quickly saw action in that war and again in the Korean War. She had nine 16-inch guns, each capable of hurling a shell weighing a ton over 20 miles.

Sidelined in 1958, *Wisconsin* was brought back into service briefly during the Gulf War.

On the chilly morning of December 7, 2000, thousands gathered along the Norfolk and Portsmouth waterfronts to watch the proud old battleship towed on her last trip. They had come from the Hampton Roads area, of course, but also from all over the United States: active and retired naval personnel who had served onboard, scrubbed her teak decks, fired her mighty guns. Some wore ancient uniforms. Some walked on board briskly; others limped from age and war-related wounds. They shared memories of serving on *Wisconsin* and nodded when the mayor of Norfolk said, "This is not now, nor will it ever be, our ship. We are only the caretakers for you."

Four tugs turned the 887-foot ship and nudged her into place in front of Nauticus, Norfolk's museum of all things of the sea. Unlike active-duty ships that go to sea to ride out storms, *Wisconsin* is not likely to ever move again, so she had to be tied down with heavy-duty chains. After two days of tours, *Wisconsin* was closed for further refurbishing until her grand reopening in April 2001.

A Potpourri of Virginia Facts

* Virginia was named for Elizabeth I of England, who never married and was called the Virgin Queen.

* Virginia comprises 42,627 square miles and has 342 miles of coastline on the mainland and 225 miles on islands.

* Virginia is shaped roughly like a triangle and is 440 miles long east to west and 196 miles north to south. Its geographic center is in Appomattox County.

* The state motto is *Sic Semper Tyrannis,* which means "Thus always to tyrants." It was selected in 1776 when Virginia and the other twelve colonies declared independence from the English king.

* At 5,719 feet, Mt. Rogers, in Smyth and Grayson Counties, is the highest peak in the state. It is in The Grayson Highlands Park.

* Virginia's state bird is the cardinal.

* Virginia's state flower is the dogwood.

* Northampton County, on the Eastern Shore, has the oldest continuous court records in America, dating to 1632.

* Virginia's official name is the Commonwealth of Virginia. Three other states—Massachusetts, Kentucky, and Pennsylvania—are also designated commonwealths.

* Six states—Kentucky, Ohio, Illinois, Indiana, Wisconsin, and part of Minnesota—were formed from land that used to be claimed by Virginia. In 1863 the northwestern counties of Virginia broke off to form the state of West Virginia.

* Eight U.S. presidents were born in Virginia: George Washington, Thomas Jefferson, James Madison, James Monroe, William Henry Harrison, John Tyler, Zachary Taylor, and Woodrow Wilson.

* Virginia's governor serves a four-year term and cannot succeed himself or herself. Mills Godwin served one term as a Democrat, then later was elected to a term as a Republican.

* Jamestown, Virginia, founded in 1607, was the first permanent English settlement in America.

* The College of William and Mary, chartered in 1693, is the second oldest college in America.

* Virginia's capital is Richmond.

* Virginia's nickname is "The Old Dominion." When Oliver Cromwell overthrew the English monarchy and beheaded Charles I, Virginia offered sanctuary to Charles II. His followers were called Cavaliers. When he became king in 1660, he referred to Virginia as his "old dominion." Because of this, Virginia is also called the Cavalier State, and the University of Virginia sports teams are called the Cavaliers.

* Two of Virginia's counties, Accomac and Northampton, on the Delmarva Peninsula, are physically joined to the rest of the state only by the Chesapeake Bay Bridge-Tunnel.

* Virginia's main agricultural products are tobacco, peanuts, soybeans, cotton, and Christmas trees.

* Virginia's population in 2000 was nearly seven million.

Bibliography

Books

Baker, Donald P. *Wilder: Hold Fast to Dreams*. Cabin John, MD: Seven Locks Press, 1989.

Blum, Howard. *I Pledge Allegiance*. New York: Simon & Schuster, 1987.

Bruce, Philip Alexander. *History of Virginia, Volume I, Colonial Period 1607–1763*. Chicago: American Historical Society, 1924.

Butt, Marshall. *Portsmouth Under Four Flags 1752–1870*. Portsmouth, VA: Portsmouth Historical Association, 1971.

Casson, Herbert. *Cyrus Hall McCormick: His Life and Work*. Chicago: A. C. McClung & Co., 1909.

Catton, Bruce. *A Stillness at Appomattox*. Garden City, NY: Doubleday, 1954.

Dabney, Virginius. *Richmond, The Story of a City*. Charlottesville: The University Press of Virginia, 1990.

———.*Virginia, The New Dominion*. Garden City, NY: Doubleday & Co., 1971.

Daniel, J. R. V. *A Hornbook of Virginia History*. Richmond, VA: Department of Conservation and Development, 1949.

Daniels, Jonathon. *The Randolphs of Virginia*. Garden City, NY: Doubleday & Co., 1972.

Davis, Julia. *The Shenandoah*. New York: Rinehart & Co., 1945.

Davis, Kenneth. *Don't Know Much About the Civil War*. New York: Avon Books, 1992.

Earley, Pete. *Family of Spies*. New York: Bantam Books, 1988.

Egerton, Douglas R. *Gabriel's Rebellion*. Chapel Hill, NC: University of North Carolina Press, 1993.

Farrar, Emmie, and Emilee Hines. *Old Virginia Houses: The Heart of Virginia*. Richmond VA: Hale Publishing, 1974.

_____. *Old Virginia Houses: The Mountain Empire*. Charlotte, NC: Delmar Co., 1978.

Garraty, John A. *The American Nation*. New York: Harper & Row, 1966.

Gill, Harold B., Jr., and Ann Finlayson. *Colonial Histories: Virginia*. Nashville, TN: Thomas Nelson Co., 1973.

Gills, Mary Louise. *It Happened at Appomattox*. Richmond, VA: The Dietz Press, 1948.

Hatch, Charles E., Jr. *The First Seventeen Years: Virginia 1607–1624*. Williamsburg, VA: Virginia 350th Anniversary Celebration, 1957.

Hobbs, Kermit, and William A. Paquette. *Suffolk: A Pictorial History*. Norfolk, VA: The Donning Co., 1987.

Hunter, Robert W., and Lynn Dean Hunter. *Spy Hunter*. Annapolis, MD: Naval Institute Press, 1999.

Kegley, F. B. *Kegley's Virginia Frontier*. Roanoke, VA: Southwest Virginia Historical Society, 1938.

McCormick, Cyrus. *The Century of the Reaper*. New York: Houghton & Mifflin Co., 1931.

McDowell, Bart. *The Revolutionary War*. Washington, DC: The National Geographic Society, 1967.

Meyers, Jeffrey. *Edgar Allan Poe: His Life and Legacy*. New York: Charles Scribner's Sons, 1992.

Moon, William Arthur. *Peter Francisco, the Portuguese Patriot.* Pfafftown, NC: Colonial Publishers, 1980.

Reynolds, Patrick, and Tom Shachtman. *The Gilded Leaf.* Boston: Little, Brown & Co., 1989.

Ryden, Hope. *America's Last Wild Horses.* New York: E. P. Dutton & Co., 1970.

Selby, John. *Stonewall Jackson.* London: B. T. Batsford, Ltd., 1968.

Stanard, Mary Newton. *The Story of Virginia's First Century.* Philadelphia: J. B. Lippincott, 1928.

State Historical Markers of Virginia. Richmond: Virginia Association of Realtors, 1975.

Swift, Earl. *When the Rain Came.* Norfolk, VA: Landmark Communications, 1999.

Thom, James Alexander. *Follow the River.* New York: Ballantine Books, 1981.

Tompkins, Edmund Pendleton. *Rockbridge County, Virginia* Richmond, VA: Whittet & Shepperson, 1952.

Tyler, Lyon Gardiner. *History of Virginia, Volume II, The Federal Period 1763–1861.* Chicago: The American Historical Society, 1924.

Viemeister, Peter. *The Beale Treasure: A History of a Mystery.* Bedford, VA: Hamilton's Press, 1987.

Wood, William, and Ralph Henry Gabriel. *The Pageant of America: The Winning of Freedom.* New Haven, CT: Yale University Press, 1927.

Magazine and Newspaper Articles

"Barter Theater—A Brief History." Abingdon, VA: Abingdon Convention and Visitors Bureau, 2000.

Berti-Camp, Laurie. "Virginia Find May Be Earliest Settlement." *The Virginian-Pilot,* April 5, 2000.

Bushnell, David. "Miss Minnie's Secret Was Worth Millions." *The Virginian Pilot-Ledger Star,* December 14, 1980.

Clancy, Paul. "The Wisconsin—Home Again." *The Virginian-Pilot,* December 7, 2000.

Crawford, Alan Pell. "A House Called Bizarre." *The Washington Post,* November 26, 2000.

Davis, Burke. "The Swinging Sweeneys." *The Iron Worker* (Autumn 1969).

Dellinger, Paul. "Chiswell Got the Lead Out." *The Roanoke Times,* April 4, 1976.

Dorsey, Jack. "Hampton Roads Goes to War—World War II 50 Years." *The Virginian-Pilot,* December 21, 1991.

"Edgar Allan Poe at Fort Monroe." *Tales of Old Fort Monroe,* Number 3. Fort Monroe: Casemate Museum, 1972.

"Five New Polio Cases in Wytheville." *The Roanoke Times,* July 12, 1950.

Flanders, Alan. "Spinster Found to Be Master Embezzler." *The Virginian-Pilot,* August 14, 1988.

Gaines, William H. "The Fatal Lamp, or Panic at the Play." *Virginia Cavalcade* (Spring 1952).

———. "The McCormick Reapers." *Virginia Cavalcade* (Summer 1954).

Grenert, Jody. "Hail to the Fleet." *The Virginian-Pilot,* May 14, 2000.

Harrison, M. Cifford. "Murder in the Courtroom." *Virginia Cavalcade* (Summer 1967).

"Home Treatment Program Helping to Care for Polio Victims After They Are Released from Hospital Ward." *The Roanoke Times,* August 4, 1950.

Jones, Matthew. "Workers Put Final Touches on Wisconsin." *The Virginian-Pilot,* December 7, 2000.

Jordan, Phyllis. "All Worked to Hide Hampton Roads During War." *The Virginian-Pilot,* December 28, 1991.

Meehan, James. "Bojangles of Richmond." *Virginia Cavalcade* (Winter 1978).

Meyer, Megan. "Saltwater Cowboys." *The Virginian-Pilot,* July 26, 2000.

"Pastures Fenced by the Sea." *Virginia Cavalcade* (Summer 1955).

"Polio Subsides in Wythe." *The Roanoke Times,* July 13, 1950.

"Ponies of Chincoteague." *Virginia* (Spring-Summer 2000).

Rachal, William M. E. "Walled Fortress and Resort Hotels." *Virginia Cavalcade* (Summer 1952).

Sawyer, W. Thomas, Jr. "The Day Hampton Roads Watched World War II." *The Virginian-Pilot,* July 3, 1997.

Sullivan, Frank. "Two U.S. Merchant Ships Torpedoed Before Eyes of Thousands." *Norfolk Virginian-Pilot,* June 17 1942.

"The Peanut King." *Virginia Cavalcade* (Summer 1958).

"Three Deaths Added to Toll." *The Roanoke Times,* August 5, 1950.

Troubetzkoy, Ulrich. "From Sophocles to Arthur Miller: The Barter Theater of Virginia." *Virginia Cavalcade* (Summer 1960).

Watson, E. Alban, and Lucille McWane Watson. "Lynchburg Tobacco Imprints." *The Iron Worker* (Winter 1950–1951).

Index

About the Author

A native Virginian and currently a freelance writer, **Emilee Hines** taught history, English, and creative writing for thirty-two years. A historian by training, with a master's degree from the University of North Carolina at Chapel Hill, she continues to be fascinated by learning new things about this oldest state. Emilee is co-author of seven volumes of *Old Virginia Houses* and author of over 250 published articles and short stories. She has traveled widely in the United States and abroad and now lives in Portsmouth, Virginia, with her husband, Thomas B. Cantieri. They have a daughter, Catherine.